# Pat & Kirby
# Go to Hell

# Pat & Kirby
# Go to Hell

Robert Kirby & Pat Bagley

SLICKROCK
BOOKS

# DEDICATION

This book is dedicated to all
who understand that the true first principle
of the gospel in this life is fear of the next.

Ever wonder if you aren't already dead and the life you're living IS your eternal reward? If so, you need this book.

Damnation duo Robert Kirby and Pat Bagley are at it again, taking the gospel zombies to task for a multitude of spiritual crimes; specifically terminal boredom and aggravated narrow-mindedness.

*Pat & Kirby Go to Hell* further rounds out the Mormon sub-standard works begun with *Sunday of the Living Dead* and *Wake Me for the Resurrection*.

It is the latest zing thrown into the cosmic melodrama that is Utah and Mormonism, a lighthearted and occasionally light-minded look at the doings and don'ts of Heavenly Father's most peculiar children.

Written for Mormons and non-Mormons—as well those traveling in both directions in between—the work contained herein makes no attempt to reconcile the way Mormon things are and the way they ought to be. That's Heavenly Father's job.

Instead, this book is offered as an antidote for folding chair blues, Sunday School drones, and church meetings that seem to compete with the Millennium. Taken in moderation, it will perk you and blow the cobwebs out of your mind. It might even drive you nuts.

Whether you agree or not with what you read here, it's guaranteed to make you think. And laugh. Which, when you think about it, is better than nodding off.

—*the publishers*

# DROPPING IN ON HELL

LAST NIGHT, I DREAMED THAT PAT AND I WENT to hell. While it may have been a vision, I'm hoping that it was just the pepperoni and peanut butter pizza. No way do I want to believe that hell is really that scary.

I've always been led to believe that the bottomless pit was either a lake of fire in which one burned forever or a cold, cheerless place of dark misery. To our horror, Pat and I soon discovered that it was much worse.

We started at the Judgment Bar which, contrary to popular opinion, isn't run by God, but rather by a committee of elderly women. This, by the way, is much scarier than being judged by God. At least with God there's a flow of logic that you can follow.

Neither of us had been particularly bad on earth. We certainly hadn't killed anybody. Still, there were those darn sins of omission. Pat routinely forgot to shave and get his hair cut, while I never really got around to doing 100 percent of my home teaching.

Anyway, the old ladies took one look at Pat's beard and yanked a lever, dropping him through the floor. However, because of my crimes against

Mormondom as committed in the *Salt Lake Tribune*, I was worked over by a couple of large angels and then flung out a window.

Getting punched out didn't bother me as much as seeing other people go right into heaven, people I thought for sure would be going to hell: insurance reps, lawyers, realtors, editors and my bishop.

Instead of a lake of fire, Pat and I landed hard in the middle of downtown Delta, Utah. Relieved that it wasn't Barstow, California, we were dusting ourselves off when Satan walked up wearing a Mr. Mac suit and loafers. He carried a briefcase rather than a pitchfork.

"Pat. Kirb," Satan said. "Welcome to hell. We've been expecting you. Take a look around and get settled. You start work tomorrow." Before we could ask about work, Satan hurried off to a meeting with Mr. Rogers and Wayne Newton.

The first thing that Pat and I did was tally up all the positive things about hell. First, there didn't appear to be any cops. Second, our clothes weren't on fire. Third, we saw Hillary Clinton kidney punching Nancy Reagan in front of McDonald's. Best of all, 7-11 had free diet Coke.

"This might be OK," Pat said, looking around.

"No," I replied. "This is very bad."

At that moment I had noticed that everyone in town was driving used Yugos. Worse, every intersection had a stoplight. Between the intersections, everyone was running over skunks.

The theaters were operating, all of them showing *Rocky IV*. The restaurants were open, but all were run by Weight Watchers. Alarmed, Pat and I borrowed a car and hit 14 skunks while driving out to the city limits where we found a sign with arrows pointing in every direction, all of which read: "Delta—7 miles."

Depressed, we drove back into town where we eventually found cartoonist Cal Grondahl selling snow skis and Postum in the park. Cal, who was only in hell on a mandatory thousand year bit, gave us the run down.

It turned out that hell had religious freedom. Sacrament meeting, Mass, and Bible study lasted seven hours every Monday, Wednesday and Friday. On Saturday, there was a rodeo, but it consisted only of drunks taking turns riding Rush Limbaugh. Every Sunday, Satan bore witness the entire day as to the truthfulness of "The Seven Habits of Highly Effective People."

It got worse. Pat and I could date in Hell, but only each other. We also had to live with our parents. Television in Hell consisted of just two channels, one showing *Barney*, the other O.J. Simpson trial reruns, both with poor horizontal hold. Lawrence Welk rap was the only music allowed.

I woke up when I discovered that my job in hell was writing missionary tracts forever. It was slightly better than Pat's job of drawing smiley faces on the top of Steven R. Covey's head.

The dream served its purpose. No way do I want to go to hell. If Church leaders would have simply told me all this stuff in the beginning, I would have been good all along.

# BROTHERS IN HARMS

I DON'T ACTUALLY HAVE TO GO TO HELL TO UNDER-
stand that the devil and I are close friends.
Although I've never seen him in the flesh, so to
speak, about ten times a day Beelzebub hints that life
would be much better if I got drunk, drove my pickup
across the neighbor's lawn and/or shot a few politicians.

I'd like to be able to say that I never listen to
Satan anymore but the truth is that I do. Fortunately,
however, I rarely take his advice. Not because Satan
doesn't sometimes make wonderful sense, but

5

because I'm a lot less scared of going to hell than I am of getting divorced.

It didn't used to be that way. Satan and I were serious pals when I was younger. Along with the usual misleading advice on drugs, sex and rock and roll, Satan also convinced me that I was a liberal, smarter than God and bullet-proof.

I'm older now and have a clearer view of Satan—namely, that he's a jerk. I've told him so

plenty of times but he still keeps coming around. I used to think it was because I was a wimp. Anymore, I think it's because we're related.

It's true. Mormons believe that Satan, like Jesus, is also our brother. It may sound crazy but it could explain a lot. Like the fact that the worst kind of trouble is always family trouble.

Jesus is a nice, responsible elder brother, the sort of elder brother who would take you places, loan you money, and teach you how to drive a stick and throw a slider. Furthermore, Jesus is always there for you.

Not Old Scratch. He's the kind of older brother who, when not giving you swirlies in the toilet or pantsing you in front of the neighbor girl, will talk you into putting the dog in the dryer for twenty minutes with the assurance that "Mom and Dad will never find out."

Satan is never there for you years later, especially when you've developed some serious antisocial problems and Muttley still swerves to the left and bashes into a wall whenever he goes after the mailman.

As famous as Lucifer is, few people recognize the devil immediately when he shows up. Incidentally, these are usually the same people who think they know what Jesus will look like when he shows up. This confusion probably explains most of Christianity's more boneheaded excesses.

Based on what I've seen at the movies and been taught at church, the devil is supposed to look like a cross between Andy Griffith and Ozzy Osbourne, with maybe a little Richard Chamberlain tossed in for sophistication.

Personally, I think Satan looks exactly like Wilford Brimley. I think this because Wilford, the straight-talking, down-to-earth guy on the Quaker Oats commercial, once talked me into buying Quaker Oats even though I hate hot cereal. But also because I don't like to think I'm stupid enough to let someone who looks like Alice Cooper convince me that setting fire to an orphanage is the best idea I ever had.

Nope, in order for him to be effective, the devil has to look like someone you'd trust. In the interest of gender equality, I'd say that's either Wilford Brimley or Aunt Bee, with maybe a little Christian Coalition chief Ralph Reed added for media savoir faire.

On the other hand, Satan could look exactly like the devilishly handsome picture at the top of this column. You never know.

# Combat Fatigue in Heaven

I N A FEW SHORT YEARS I'LL BE STANDING BEFORE
THE Judgment Bar. God is going to expect some
answers for the way I've behaved down here. Up
until last week, I didn't have any. At least none that
sounded good. Heretofore, my best excuse had been
a shrug and "just because."

Pretty lame excuse for a lifetime of spiritual and
temporal crimes. For the last forty or so years, I've
been belligerent, stressed, cynical, arrested, testified
against (both in church and out) and plagued with

indecent thoughts about Michelle Pfeiffer. None of these, incidentally, has been entirely my fault.

I blame it on combat. More specifically, Post-Traumatic Stress Disorder suffered long before I was born. Hey, the War in Heaven was tough on some of us.

As you know, God's children fought a war in the pre-existence. It resulted in a 33 1/3 percent casualty rate, including the supreme commander of the opposing force, Satan. It wasn't a pretty sight. I lost a lot of friends, thirty-three and a third to be exact.

I served with the elite Alpha & Omega First Division (airborne). For three eons, we went head-to-head with Satan's best: the Eighteenth Corruption Corps and elements of two Damnation Armored Brigades. I'll never forget it.

For those who survived, our reward for those terrible times was life here on earth. No parade, no praise, just an ignominious birth and an attempt to blot what happened from our minds. God placed a veil on our minds so that we wouldn't remember it.

But pain won't be denied. I can't forget Doc, Gunner, Smitty and Lopez, who didn't make it. Worse, there's Jake who almost bought it, getting born on earth as a dwarf in order to round out the casualty list to exactly thirty-three and a third.

To this day, I can't understand why I made it. Neither, of course, can my parents, wife, teachers, assorted bishops, and cops. Why did so many good spirits get wasted in heaven when spirits like me, Timothy Leary, Hitler, Blackbeard, and Hillary Clinton made it through? Was it fate, luck of the draw, or something else?

As with any war, not every soldier in Deseret

Storm saw combat. A lot of spirits, judging from their positions here on earth, never saw combat up there. For example, did you know that Donald Trump was a cook during the Great Cast Out Offensive? Brigham Young was a motorpool sergeant. Liz Taylor was a nurse and Elvis was a lifeguard at the Officer's Club.

But regular people like you and me were front line grunts. We saw it all. It explains our slothfulness and failure to magnify down here. PTSD keeps us from reaching our potential. When we're called to account for our lack of faithfulness, we can show our scars and say we already gave all.

Detractors of this theory say the War in Heaven wasn't really that kind of war, that it was more a big debate over who to follow: Jesus or Satan. What fighting occurred was only fighting in the figurative sense. My response, of course, is to point out the veil over our minds. If nobody really remembers, how does anyone really know what happened? I could be right.

I hope. After talking this Judgment Bar defense theory over with Pat, though I'm a bit worried. He has this crazy idea that we were both conscientious objectors during the War in Heaven.

# LIVING DEATH DOWN

WENT TO A FUNERAL LAST WEEK. NOBODY I knew. I went out of respect for a close friend whose grandmother had passed away. Bummer. The funeral, not her death. I hate them.

Frankly, when it comes to funerals, I'd rather be the one who's dead. Mainly because I don't think being dead is going to be anything worth getting upset about. It's not like you can change your mind.

Depending on how it happens, dying might be very upsetting before actual death sets in. Especially if said dying takes longer than three seconds and involves cancer, a band saw, a shark, or a lot of ants.

I've given death a lot of thought and arrived at the conclusion that I'm pro-dead but very anti-dying. For the record, however, I'm not so anti-dying that I refuse to concede the merits in brain aneurysms, big explosions, or meteorites. I don't care how, just so long as it's fast.

Or so I thought.

At Grandma Wilkerham's funeral, one of the speakers talked about death being a great reunion. Grandma, he said, was happy because she was finally reunited with loved ones who had been waiting for her.

For me, this clinched being dead. I'm looking forward to seeing some of my own friends, most notably Bruce, Mike, JoAnne and Elliot. I'd also like to reacquaint myself with my maternal grandfather, who everyone says that I'm like.

After welcoming you back, I think friends and loved ones are going to want to know what happened to you down on earth, specifically how things ended

for you. Which brings us back to dying.

See, given that there's a reunion in heaven, it's possible that how long it takes you to die isn't as important as the actual how.

My grandfather died of a heart attack. Bruce died of cancer. A passion for big street bikes got Elliot. JoAnne was murdered and Vietnam got Mike. All deaths that the recipients can be proud of.

What if mine isn't? What if I die, pardon the pun, in a manner that would be tough to live down? I bring this up because I read a news story about six people who drowned in Egypt while trying to rescue a chicken from a well.

Not only that one, but the one about a guy who lived on beans and cabbage and literally gassed himself to death one night while sleeping in an airtight bedroom. Then the one about the Toronto lawyer who fell 24 floors to his death while demonstrating the strength of the glass in his office windows to visitors. Or the Florida man killed while traveling 80-mph on Interstate 95 while trying to read a sales manual?

Just imagine your heavenly reunion with loved ones. You're chatting when someone says, "So, Ed, how'd you check out?" After Walt and John just got done talking about their Medal of Honor and valiant fight with Lou Gehrig's Disease, are you going to want to tell them about putting that can of pork and beans in the camp fire?

Cancer, brain tumors, drowning, none of that stuff scares me as bad any more. Even being a sinner doesn't scare me as bad as it once did. I've got bigger worries now.

Now that I know there's peer pressure involved in being dead, I just don't want my last earthly thought to be "that @#&! chicken."

# LET THE GOOD TIMES ROLL

I USED TO THINK THAT ANYONE WHO SAID "wickedness never was happiness" didn't really know wickedness. I've been wicked most of my life and I can tell you that it's damn fun. Literally.

Alas, I go to a church that teaches "man is that he might have joy." We've used this "joy" phrase for so long that the word has lost all meaning. What is joy? If we're all individuals, wouldn't joy be an individual thing?

Frankly, I rather enjoy being bad. Mainly because being bad isn't as boring as being good. Unless, of course, you get caught. Then you go to prison which, I'm told, is way up there on the unenjoyable/boring chart. The only times prison ever gets exciting is when wicked things happen that make you really unhappy.

Sadly, being wicked comes with a price other than going to prison. Be wicked enough and you could go to

hell which, according to Sunday School, is very bad. When it comes to cellmates, I'd much rather room with a tattooed guy named Bubba than I would Satan.

Wickedness means doing pretty much what you want. The whole point of being evil is the thrill of feeling the wind in your hair. Being a slave to your passions isn't all that bad. It's got to be better than being a slave to someone else's passions.

Which brings us to being good. Righteousness seems to entail doing whatever someone else tells you to do, whether it's folding your arms in Sunday School or forking over large sums of money.

Suffice it to say then that I'm a little fuzzy on this whole heaven/hell thing. From paintings of both, I gather that heaven is full of clouds while hell is full

17

of fire. Such an overly simple explanation may suffice for most people, but not people like me. We're quick to point out that tornados and monsoons have clouds, too, but that doesn't make them great places to be. Conversely, a roaring fire can be quite nice on a cold night.

Mormons claim to have answers to these confusing issues, mainly that things get reversed when we die. In heaven, unlike on earth, we can do whatever we want: wander a limitless meadow or surf a comet through the universe, sit at the feet of God or run over cats. OK, not the cat thing.

Hell is where someone else gets to tell us what to do and think. Worse, there's no parole date. Somehow, I don't think hell's priorities include entertainment. If you really want to know what hell is like, imagine church for time and all eternity.

Maybe church has got it all wrong then. Maybe the next time the bishop/pastor/priest gets up, the message really ought to be, "What we're doing right now, people, is what it's going to be like forever if we don't behave."

I don't know about you, but that would certainly scare the hell out of me.

This role reversal between heaven and earth can make you wonder if God isn't schizophrenic. Or it might, if not for the fact that God loves us and wants us to thrive. Like life, heaven and hell are all about options.

Makes sense. Selfishly doing whatever you want tends to narrow your focus and therefore your options. Self-control, on the other hand, teaches people how to manage the unlimited freedom God promises us once we've learned how to behave.

# REIGNING CATS AND DOGS

I F GOD HAS A PET, AND I BELIEVE THAT HE DOES, IT
has to be a dog. Not a pure breed, either. The God
I believe in owns a mutt, a big, slobbering thing
with the heart of a lion and the brain of a marble.

As you might expect, the subject of God having a
dog is a sensitive one with most people. Not only do
most people refuse to believe that God has a pet, but
those who might consider it also figure that if he
does, no way would it be a dog.

The few people I've met who conceded the
God/pet issue have invariably argued for a more noble
pet type: elephant, tiger, whale, T-Rex and, in one
bizarre case, a mongoose. These people were all idiots.

Over the years, I have argued this deep theological issue with pastors, bishops, reverends, priests, and
at least one rabbi. None of them were ever able to
convince me of the truthfulness of their faith because

none of them ever conceded that God would have a dog. One came close.

"All of God's creations are in effect his pets," said a minister who almost had me. "So I suppose it could be reasonably argued that God has a dog for a pet. Yes, I'm sure of it."

"OK, then, what's the dog's name?"

"Well, I don't really see—"

"Liar!"

A dog is the sort of pet God would have. You don't need to look it up in the Bible. Just think about it for a minute. Dogs love unconditionally. Dogs are loyal. Dogs are brave. You see dogs in *Reader's Digest* all the time rescuing people. Dogs have the spirit of truth in them, in part because they aren't smart enough to know how to lie.

By the way, God's dog is named Vern.

This is not your typical religious subject, I know. It's an important one to me because I had to put my dog to sleep last week. Pig, my dog, collapsed with heat exhaustion during a hike in the mountains and suffered irreparable kidney damage.

The only thing that has sustained me during the last few days is the belief that when I die, Pig will be there waiting for me. She may be bathed in celestial glory but she'll still be my unlicensed, gopher-digging, rug-gnawing best friend.

I'm a Mormon but my wants are simple. God can keep the celestial mansion, eternal glory and everything else. Pig was family. If families really are forever, then I want her back.

Actually, I want all of my former dogs back. Pig, Lennon, Beau, John Wayne, Baron and Lurch. If I'm good, God will give them back to me because, frankly, heaven would be pretty pointless without them.

Wait. I probably won't get Beau back. Not unless I go to hell. I'm pretty sure that's where he is. Beau was not a good dog. I'm not talking about the time he tore the pants off a terrified Jehovah's Witness either. Beau's moral turpitude involved cats. He liked them. He hung out with them.

It doesn't take the pope or a prophet to point out the fact that cats are deceitful and nasty. They are stiff-necked and arrogant, puffed up in their pride. Cats are cruel, evil things utterly incapable of loyalty and honor. Ever see a cat rescue someone from drowning? Nope. And that's why you won't ever see a cat in heaven.

The devil has a cat for a pet. It's name is Princess.

# FELINE FORGIVENESS

ONE OF THE HARDEST THINGS I'VE EVER HAD to do as a practicing (but not yet accomplished) Mormon is ask for forgiveness from people I've wronged. The Church says it's an absolute essential part of the gospel plan.

I'm hoping that God isn't a real stickler on this one. Not because I hate to ask for forgiveness, but rather because I doubt that I could locate all the people I've ever wronged. We're probably talking billions.

I've asked for forgiveness approximately 50 times during my life. Incidentally, this was about noncoerced forgiveness. Not the "I'll-go-to-hell-if-I-don't" kind.

For example, I don't count begging for forgiveness from cops, judges, the IRS, and my wife. Begging for forgiveness so that a loan shark won't have someone pull your nose off with a pair of vise grips is self-preservation, not repentance. As such, God probably doesn't count it.

The forgiveness I'm talking about is the forgiveness you want because you injured someone and you feel bad about it. For example, when I was young, I accidentally drove my car onto the neighbor's lawn, smashing a ceramic donkey and a birdbath. When I said I was sorry, the neighbor forgave me.

Since restitution is part of repentance and forgiveness, I paid for the damage. There are, of course, some sins so huge that you can't make complete restitution here on earth. Stuff like murder, embezzlement, and voting for Ross Perot. In cases like this, you just do the best you can and hope that God will

make up the difference.

I'm going somewhere with all of this. Namely, another plea for forgiveness. As you may already know, I've not been exactly kind to cats in this column. Recently, I claimed that Satan had a cat for a pet instead of a way cool dog named Vern like God has.

In the space of a week, I got a short ton of letters from cat lovers, most of whom were so offended by what I wrote that they put aside their Christianity and demanded I be ground up for kitty litter.

However, a few people (cat lovers) presented their opposing views in such a way that I felt somewhat bad for saying that all cats would go to hell.

So, here goes: I'm sincerely sorry for what I wrote about cats. What I really meant to say was that MOST cats would go to hell, but probably not yours. Those of you who screeched for my head can go pound sand. Your cats are going to hell even if I have to take them there myself.

OK, I'm sorry I said that, too. Please forgive me. Again.

What's really cool about asking for forgiveness is that it automatically puts the ball in the offended person's court. I like this part. See, Jesus not only wants us to ask for forgiveness, he also wants us to forgive other people.

Believe it or not, forgiving other people is even tougher than asking them to forgive you. A sense of self-righteous anger is the only thing that gets most people out of bed in the morning. If I couldn't hate at least five hundred people a day, I wouldn't know what to do with myself.

I better work on it though. God knows what to do with me if I don't. I'll be somewhere keeping your cat company.

# DOG DAZE IN THE FIELD

I'VE BEEN COMING HOME FROM CHURCH IN A BAD mood for more than 40 years. Admittedly, most of the fault is mine. I'm easily bored. The rest of the fault belongs to church. It's easily boring.

If the gospel really is the greatest thing on earth, can somebody explain why learning about it is like being force fed dry toast? What's the point of going to Sunday School when you already know what the answers will be?

Frankly, conversations where everyone already agrees can be a dangerous thing. Do it long enough and eventually the touch of the Master's hand becomes indistinguishable from a dart full of animal tranquilizer.

Maybe I was born in the wrong time. I'm thinking that I would have been better off living during Old Testament times. Learning about the gospel by watching Sister Frapp get turned into a salt lick or a whale swallow my bishop would have been cool.

Getting and keeping people's attention about religion can be a daunting job. I did it full-time for two years on an LDS mission. I learned how hard it is to encourage people bored with their own church to come to your church when you know it's boring, too.

But who says the gospel has to be boring? Well, in the Mormon church, the correlation committee does, that's who. Fortunately, they were in Salt Lake City in 1975 when the president of the Uruguay Mission encouraged us to get around people's natural indifference by coming up with new ways to present the gospel.

The president probably meant stuff like street displays, small media events, and interesting door presentations. I decided that what he really meant was a big mangy dog.

The dog in question was Lurch, a big German shepherd/ greyhound mix who had adopted Elder Carl English of New Jersey and me. Tired of being ignored by the people of a small beach town, English and I set about changing our luck.

We dressed Lurch in a white shirt, gym shorts, necktie and name tag, and took him tracting. Lurch couldn't speak Spanish and he wasn't set apart, but nobody ignored him.

English and I took turns hiding. People answered their doors to find two Mormon missionaries, one decidedly uglier than the other, standing beside two bikes. The double takes were priceless.

It wasn't all fun. Generally speaking, people don't expect Mormon missionaries to bite the heads off their cats. Lurch was also hard on our white shirts. One of English's was ripped to pieces in a dog fight while one of mine had to be burned after it came home smelling like something dead.

Me and my smartest Companion

Mostly, though, it was great. People stopped ignoring us and started waving when we passed by. They became less gruff when we rang their doors at inopportune times. After about a month of this, Lurch could have gotten elected mayor of San Jose de Carrasco.

This story should end with a multitude of baptisms. It doesn't. Sure, we made a few converts. There are probably still one or two people down there who can claim that a dog taught them the gospel in the summer of '75.

Alas, the assistants to the president showed up and told us to quit tracting with Lurch. They said it was "dangerous" to give people the wrong idea about the Church.

The moral? I don't have one. Only that if people can make religion boring, they can also make it interesting.

# MIRACLE WHIPPED

EARLY ALL RELIGIONS ASCRIBE TO MIRACLES and visions as proof of God and their own divine mandate. Catholics have their sightings of the Virgin Mary. Mormons believe Joseph Smith saw God. Meanwhile, another faith claims that crystals will cure acne and piles.

Then everyone argues about whose miracle was better.

Although cynical by nature, I happen to believe in miracles. Raising the dead, healing the blind, turning water into wine, I'm convinced that Jesus really did all of that stuff.

I used to wonder why. I mean if the point of a miracle is to do good, how come Jesus didn't cleanse all the lepers instead of just a few? After all, if a little bit

of good is wonderful, a lot of good has to be even better, right?

The conclusion I've come to is that miracles have
less to do with seemingly random acts of divine gen-
erosity than they do with God trying to get the
attention of a few idiots. And the dumber you are,
the bigger the miracle has to be.

I've only witnessed two possible miracles. The
first occurred in 1972 when a tank almost squashed a
jeep I was driving in Georgia. I was just tooling along
in the night and suddenly there was this tank coming
the opposite way.

I have no idea how we missed each other. All I know is that in a flash the tank was past me, snorting and clanking on down the trail. Oh, and that going to the bathroom in your pants does not necessarily detract from the effects of a religious experience.

The second happened in 1975 when God cast out an attractive woman's mind long enough for her to agree to marry me. Of the two, the latter has had more lasting effect. While the tank has faded to a dim but disturbing memory, Irene is just in the other room, apparently still willing to live on what I drag home.

Anyway, God got my attention both times. I rarely bring this up because it's a little hard to explain to people why I consider these events personal miracles. You had to be there and be me in order to appreciate them.

The big miracle of record in Utah is the one about the sea gulls. When Mormon pioneers were starving in 1848, a plague of crickets came to the valley and started eating everything in sight. Mormons believe that God saved them by sending a gob of sea gulls.

The story goes that the birds flew in and chowed down. When they got full, the gulls flew over to Salt Lake, threw up (see above reference to bodily functions and miracles) and came back for more. Everyone cheered because the crops were saved and Utah was introduced to the buffet concept.

Skeptics will point out that this wasn't a real miracle because it was something birds and bugs do naturally. A better miracle would have been God sending bears to eat Johnston's army. After all, when it comes to attention getting, birds eating bugs isn't all that hot. Now a horde of bears eating a regiment of cavalry and a federal judge . . .

That's the problem with miracles. They never happen in such a way that banishes all doubt, particularly among the skeptics. On the other hand, the overly devout sometimes see miracles where there really weren't any.

When it comes right down to it, maybe what's really important is what miracles do for you personally rather than what they do for everyone else.

# Tongue-Tied

I BECAME A MORMON BACK IN 1961, WHEN MY father baptized me in a swimming pool near Zaragoza, Spain.

Being the kind of kid I was and eventually became, Dad still insists that it was more of an exorcism than anything else. Maybe that's why the longest stretch of time I've ever encountered in life was the three minutes I spent underwater in that pool.

Anyway, I've been a Mormon for 36 years. In that time I've seen or participated in most aspects of the church. Everything from mission field dysentery to Sunday School lessons extolling the virtues of the John Birch Society.

There is one thing, however, that I've never seen done. Despite having heard a lot of things in church that didn't always make sense, I've never actually heard anyone speak in tongues.

Why is that? I mean it's right there in the seventh Article of Faith: "We believe in the gift of tongues . . ." If we believe in it, where is it? Mormons apparently did it all the time back in Missouri and Nauvoo.

When I was learning the Articles of Faith as a kid, old number seven made me more than a little nervous. Up until then, the only thing I had to compare it to was the time my parents killed a pig and made a gift of its head to our Spanish landlord.

Whereas I could handle the "laying on of hands" and even baptism by long emersion, giving away tongues was more that I was willing to bargain for. I vowed then and there to be just enough of a sinner so that I would never have to worry about it.

It was a vow I kept. Not once in the 36 years have I heard anyone in church suddenly hold forth in a language that I didn't understand or at least recognize as an earthly form of communication.

On the other hand, it's possible that I have heard tongues spoken but was just too spiritually dense to realize it. For example, I heard a talk a while back that could have been uttered in tongues.

I distinctly remember Brother Hooper saying "the geographical center of Zion is on my cousin's farm exactly two miles east of Kanab." While it sounded like plain English, it could have been tongues for, "I'm a dangerous idiot. Please throw a net over me." Unless Brother Hooper and his cousin turn up in the news surrounded by ATF agents, we'll probably never know for sure.

When I was in the army, I heard people bellow in tongues. Obviously it wasn't a Mormon thing though. Usually the person doing the bellowing had to be at least a buck sergeant and very upset about something to do with anomalies in my immediate family history.

Although he's not a Mormon, I've also seen television evangelist Robert Tilton speak in tongues. Bob will be rambling on about how much it costs to

preach the gospel when suddenly, right out of the blue, he starts into something which can only be described by sensible people as gospel ebonics.

"Yama-oolay-haggis-poot," Tilton will say with a perfectly straight face. Which, depending on your level of spirituality, means either "yama-oolay-haggis-poot" or "send me lots of money, you fools."

That's the trouble with tongues. You just never know. On the other hand, it's also the plus. See, if my bishop called me to a position, and I said "yes," how would he know it wasn't tongues for "Get real?"

Seriously, I've read where people spoke in tongues during Biblical times. As such, I'm willing to concede that it has and can still be done (in the spiritual sense). I've just never understood the bother. If God wants people to know something so important, why put it in code?

# SALVATION: IT TAKES A BRAIN

WHILE SPEAKING TO A RELIGIOUS GROUP several months ago, someone in the audience asked if I believed Gordon B. Hinckley was a prophet of God. I said yes.

"So does that mean that if Hinckley told you to kill someone you would?"

The answer to that, of course, was no. I don't do crazy stuff just because someone else tells me to, even if they are a prophet. I have enough trouble with my own brain telling me to runover people just because they cut me off in traffic.

I actually get a lot of bad ideas that make perfect sense, which is probably why I believe in prophets. In fact, if it wasn't for Jesus and prophets laying out God's will so that even dolts like me could follow it,

I'd probably be on death row.

The optimist in me says that the world needs prophets. The skeptic says that not everyone who claims to be a link between man and God is actually such a thing. For example, some of the money grubbing, widow robbing, Jesus screechers on television today.

The problem rests, I suppose, in who you consider to be a prophet. Also, in how blindly you decide to follow them. While I believe in prophets, I probably wouldn't have gotten along with somebody like Jim Jones or David Koresh. Especially if they wanted the deed to my house or my daughter.

Which brings me to my own church. As a Mormon, I wonder if I would have followed Brigham Young to Utah just because he said it was God's idea. A lot of Mormons didn't. Having to choose between a cozy home in Nauvoo and a 2,000 mile ride in a rickety wagon is a serious dilemma.

Following church leaders on an epic trek west is one thing. Letting them convince you to massacre a wagon train is another. Mountain Meadows serves today as a perfect reminder that though God gives us religious leaders, he also gives us brains. When one starts talking, we're not automatically commanded to stop thinking.

But this isn't just a Mormon thing. It's happened all through history. As you recall, the ancient Jewish prophet Joshua is still revered today for his "as for me and my house, we will serve the Lord" motto.

On at least one occasion, this motto meant Joshua telling his people to slaughter everyone in the city of Jericho. Not just the men, women and children, but also the donkeys, pigs and hamsters. Call me a child of darkness, but Joshua and I would have had a serious disagreement over the idea of serving God by killing little kids.

Back when I was a cop, I used to wonder what I'd do if man's law and God's law ever locked horns in a big way. Specifically, what I would have done if, while on patrol, I chanced upon the prophet

Abraham poised to sacrifice Isaac.

If God really did command Abraham to cut his son's throat, my only hope is that He would have clued me in. Otherwise, I would have capped Abraham in a heartbeat. Sacrificing people is against the law, you know.

Today there's ample evidence that the line between faithful and foolish sometimes gets a little fuzzy. When it comes to following a religious leader, you've got to keep your wits about you. Which, by the way, is rather hard to do if you turn them over to the person you're following.

# SUFFER THE
# LITTLE CHILDREN

I N CHURCH LAST WEEK, I HAD A VERY DEEP
religious conversation with Buddy. Neither of
us wanted to have the conversation but we did
anyway. Mainly because I outweigh Buddy by 200
pounds and he's only six years old.

Buddy was misbehaving in his Sunday School
class, namely jumping around like an unmedicated
lunatic and kicking over chairs, some of which were
occupied by his more docile classmates. Unable to
calm him down, the teacher sent Buddy out into the
hall to fend for himself.

This was bad for Buddy because the hall in the
Springcreek 8th Ward is the primary feeding ground of
Brother Kirby who, legend has it, once ate four kids
and their dog for no real reason.

I caught Buddy trying to hide in the bathroom. He fessed up right away that Sister Hamhips had given him the boot just because he was bored.

The Spirit moved me to explain to Buddy an important gospel principle. Getting choked isn't as tedious as yet another lesson on faith and did he want me to make things more interesting for him? A theologian in his own right, Buddy was quick to point out that Jesus never choked anybody.

Me: "Jesus never ate any little kids, either."

Buddy: "I'm supposed to be in class."

I don't know how it is in other churches, but bored kids are a big problem in nearly all Mormon wards. Frankly, it's not the kids' fault. Rather it's the fault of adult Mormons, specifically that we have so many kids that they outnumber us 40-1. Custer got better odds and look what happened to him.

If church is so stultifying to an adult, it's a million times worse for a kid who, on average, expends more calories just going to the bathroom than an entire chain gang of adults will in a week.

Here comes the problem. It's a bit unreasonable to expect kids to sit still for three hours doing the sort of things that cause adults to fall asleep. I know, I used to be a kid. Back then, the mark of the beast was any required display of reverence. Staunch Mormons left the church rather than accept a calling to be my Primary teacher. Picture Peter Pan on crack.

The problem isn't the message but rather the messengers. Most adults go to church because they have to, an incomprehensible attitude to kids. For a kid, not wanting to do something is a perfectly good reason not to do it.

Which, of course, is why kids need to learn church stuff. After all, just because giving your kid sister swimming lessons in the toilet sounds like a good idea doesn't mean that God does. However, you may not want to bring this particular item up during a lesson on Noah and the flood.

On the other hand, it's tough to teach kids about the dangers of hell when they think that they're already there. What could possibly be scarier than being seven and feeling your butt start to grow roots on a folding chair?

I'm guessing that the big problem stems from the fact that adults haven't figured out that church is too long. Despite what they hear in church, time and all eternity for Mormon kids is anything that lasts three hours.

Having been a kid, I can tell you that Sunday School is what most kids think Jesus was really talking about when he said "suffer the little children."

# TESTI-MOANING

BEARING WITNESS. MOST RELIGIONS DO IT. IT consists mainly of telling people about your faith in God, sharing your beliefs with them so that they'll be inspired by your example.

Or turned off, as the case may be. After all, bearing witness of Jesus Christ isn't in and of itself anything special or sacred. Particularly if part of your witness is the claim that Jesus told you to blow up a federal building.

For some religions, bearing witness requires a lot of alarming folderol, i.e., screeching, speaking in tongues, and flinging oneself about while wrapped in snakes. Members of other faiths bear witness by simply telling you that Jesus lives. Still others, my personal favorites, bear witness by simply behaving themselves.

I'm most familiar with Mormons witness bearing, or the bearing of testimonies. We have a meeting

44

built around it, the first Sunday of every month, when the podium is thrown open to the general congregation.

Fast and testimony meeting is viewed with a mixture of hope and dread by those in attendance. Considerable research reveals that there are only five kinds of testimonies:

PARENT PARADE—The warm up act for testimony meeting in most LDS wards is a string of small witness-bearing kids. They take turns doing chin-ups on the lectern, testifying per some secret kid script,

"I'd like to bear my testimony I know the church true I love my mom and . . . " in a single breath.

I've never really understood the logic behind the parent parade, unless it's to get kids into the habit of bearing witness about things they really don't understand. On the other hand, maybe it plants the seeds early in young minds that everything that comes from a pulpit doesn't necessarily come from God.

TESTI-MOANING—Someone, usually the same person every time, will get up and try and convince you that Jesus loves them because he's trying to kill them. They've lost their job, their kid's on drugs, their brother's gay, and a wolf bit off one of their legs to keep them from having Family Home Evening. Their testimony is a litany of woe, the conclusion of which is that life is a hideous series of emotional maimings but a special blessing nonetheless.

PARTING THE HEAVENS—Not all testimonies are such downers. Every once in awhile, someone does it for you. They'll say something that opens a door in your head and suddenly you get "it"— whatever "it" happens to be for you. This has happened to me about ten times, two of which occurred in other churches, and once on a bus.

HOLY HARANGUE—Alas, every ward has a Moses or Brigham Young wannabe. Testimony meeting is this person's time to shine. For twenty minutes, "Righteous" Limbaugh will hold forth as to why the world, the country, the state, the ward and you are so screwed up. Usually it has something to do with the media, although sometimes it's Clinton or food storage.

GOSPEL GABBER—Only the gabber can rival the haranguer when it comes to taking up testimony time. What you get here however, is a running monologue of ward rather than world trivia. Who's grateful, helpful, sorrowful, or just plain full of it in the Cramp Heights 8th Ward.

Despite what it sounds like, I'm not against the idea of people bearing their witness or their testimony. Even if you don't agree with them, it lets you know what kind of person you're dealing with. Used properly, that can be blessing enough.

# X-Commandments for Generation X

J UDGE ROY S. MOORE OF GADSEN, ALA., IS IN
trouble these days. The ACLU (Anti-Christ's
Lawyers Union, according to my dad) is mad
at the circuit court judge because he's got a wooden
plaque of the Ten Commandments hanging in his
courtroom.

The ACLU says Moore's public manifestation of
his faith is contrary to the constitutional separation
of church and state. The ACLU isn't so much worried that God will creep into the Moore's courtroom,
but that it will be Moore's version of God: to wit, a
Christian god.

I could be wrong but I always thought this country's
laws were based on the Judeo-Christian perception of
the Ten Commandments. Thank God (sue me).

Given mankind's frequently screwy notions about such things as manners and morality, it's probably a good thing that we didn't think these commandments up on our own.

On the other hand, I see the merit in the ACLU's concern (damn me) about letting a particular religion drive the government. Think about it? Say you accidentally killed somebody in a traffic accident. Would it make you feel comfortable if the judge ruling on your case had a big "eye for an eye" sign hanging behind him? What if he was a Mormon fundamentalist big on the idea of blood atonement?

Better yet, what if you were convicted of shooting and eating one of your neighbor's cows? Would it matter to you if the judge sentencing you was known for viewing the law exclusively through the prism of Hinduism? You'd be an idiot if it didn't.

The fate of Moore's Ten Commandment plaque will be decided in a legal battle which, given how legal things go, probably won't be decided until the Second Coming of Christ, at which time the ACLU can take their case all the way to the most supreme court.

Better still, how about a truce? Maybe if Moore would make his Ten Commandments more human-centered instead of God-centered, the ACLU might agree to stop suing him. Toward that end, I've come up with a revised set of Ten Commandments that should make everyone happy. Except, of course, God.

God's Ten Commandments for his '90s children.

1. Thou shalt not take the name of the Lord thy God in vain except during R-rated movies, sporting events, and Congressional hearings.

2. Six days shalt thou labor, and do all thy work. But the seventh day is the Sabbath of the Lord thy God: in it thou shalt go to a monster truck race.

3. Honor thy father and thy mother, save it be that claims that thy father mistreated thy pet gerbil might landest thou on *Oprah*.

4. Thou shalt not kill cats.

5. Thou shalt not steal, save it be from large corporations or thy federal government.

6. Thou shalt not bear false witness against thy neighbor if thou canst first secure from thy neighbor a six-figure, out-of-court settlement.

7. Thou shalt not covet thy neighbor's wife, nor

GENERATION X COMES DOWN FROM THE MOUNT...

his special man friend, nor his mistress, nor his alternate personality, nor any psycho-therapist that is thy neighbor's.

8. Thou shalt not make unto thee any graven images, save it be through liposuction, collagen injections, hair replacement and breast implants.

9. Thou shalt not commit adultery, save thou happenest to be drunk, yea exceedingly.

10. Thou shalt have no other gods before me save they be Mastercard, VISA and American Express.

# INFERNAL MARRIAGE

I T'S NO SECRET THAT MORMONS BELIEVE IN eternal marriage. The big mystery to a lot of people is why anyone would want to be married that long.

There was a time when I thought everyone would be wowed by the idea of being hitched forever. This is understandable considering that the main reason most people get married in the first place is because they're in love, even if it was an obstetrician who told them.

I mostly had this idea when I was an LDS missionary tramping around South America. Because we were the only church offering this option, my companions and I made some serious headway with "Families are Forever."

Came the day, however, that we knocked on the door of an older widow. We gave her the standard spiel and waited for her to weep with joy. Instead, she flew into a rage.

I won't quote the woman verbatim here, mainly because she was speaking Spanish but also because she used the español equivalent of "sonuvabitch" about 40 times in reference to her dead husband. It made my companion start singing a hymn.

She basically said that eternal marriage didn't sound like her idea of a heavenly reward. Her 28-year-marriage worked out to be 27 years longer than she needed to find out that her husband was a stingy,

perverted, lazy and abusive drunk. Before slamming the door, she added that the only bad feeling she had about her husband's death was that she hadn't killed him herself.

Needless to say this put a wrinkle in our gospel marketing methods. Thereafter, we weren't so quick to tell people that Mormons offered a doozy of a wedding plan. In a Catholic country where divorce was illegal, it turned out that not everyone was keen on being with their significant other forever.

However, I'm happy to point out that some good did come of this experience. When I got a "Dear John" letter from my girlfriend the following week, it didn't bother me as much as it might have before. I remember thinking, "Hey, better now than in 14.7 bajillion years."

But just because some people hate being married doesn't mean everyone else does. Plenty of people out there like the idea of being married, so much so, that eternity seems pretty pointless if they aren't going to spend it with their spouse. I'm one of them.

I've been thinking that maybe what Mormons need is an eternal marriage pre-nuptial agreement. That might make a temple marriage more attractive these days. Something like this:

"We the undersigned agree to marry for the purposes of eternity provided that in the event of a divorce, the following stipulations are adhered to jointly, individually and eternally."

* Should a divorce be sought, neither party shall retain Satan as legal counsel.

* Both parties agree not to lay legal claim to any portion of the other party's celestial reward that existed prior to the marriage.

\* The children of the union shall be divided evenly between both parties with the exception of those children currently in hell.

\* Neither party may subpoena God as a character witness.

\* The halos of both parties shall be sold and the profits therefrom divided evenly between the separating parties and their respective lawyers.

There, that oughta do it.

Then again, couples who actually get to stay together for eternity must first dump the earthly meanness that makes divorce such a land-office business in the first place.

Never mind.

# CORRELATED CLONING

LAST WEEK, I LISTENED TO LDS GENERAL conference (including the "Morm-ercials") and didn't hear the Brethren say one word on the subject of cloning.

Maybe it's because cloning people is old news to Mormons. We've been doing it for years. If you don't think so, take a drive past the Missionary Training Center in Provo some day. At a glance, you'll see hundreds of people who look, act, walk, talk and think exactly alike. It's very inspiring in an *Invasion of the Body Snatchers* sort of a way.

It's not just missionaries either. Most Mormons, at least the ones here in Utah, fit a particular mold. We're known for our white shirts, floral dresses, gang voting, Republican hair-dos and surreptitious use of diet Coke and Prozac.

Prove it to yourself. Go downtown and cull Mormons off a sidewalk based on nothing more than their appearance. You'll be right 95% of the time.

Detractors will, of course, say that this isn't real cloning. They'll argue that it's more a matter of socialization than one of genetic engineering. Out of respect to my detractors, I'd like to point out that they're all fools and morons. Everyone knows that Mormons have long experimented with DNA.

For years, the LDS church insisted that Mormons marry only other Mormons. This wasn't exactly a good idea in the early years of the Church because the Mormon gene pool was rather small. The pool is much wider today, although in some places still only about an inch deep.

Breeding out of primarily Nordic and English stock, the early Church eventually came up with the perfect Mormon look: fair-haired, blue-eyed, square-jawed, Osmond-toothed and loyal to a fault. It drove Hitler nuts.

Understandably, this experimentation was never referred to by Mormons as cloning. In an attempt to mislead the federal government, the Church called it "biological correlation." The good news is that it has largely succumbed to a more modern LDS genetics program: BYU football.

It didn't take Mormons long to learn that "white and delightsome" alone can't guarantee a WAC championship. For that, the church needed some "black and frightsome" stock, specifically black and frightsome that weighed 280 + and could run the 100 in under 10 seconds with University of Utah DNA splattered all over his helmet.

Oh, and we started sending missionaries to places

like Africa. Needless to say, this makes it much harder to clone a typical Mormon because we're fast coming to the point where there isn't going to be one. Praise God.

Still, it might be fun to dig up some early Mormons and do a little "gentile cloning" with their DNA just for laughs. I wonder how Brigham Young would do with today's LDS church?

Maybe it's better that we don't bring the old Mormons back. After all, who would want to run the risk of a John D. Lee in charge of Utah's tourism board? What about Porter Rockwell II as

Commissioner of Public Safety? Best to leave well enough alone.

There are pros and cons to cloning. On the good side, cloning would negate our old argument for polygamy. You could marry the exact same woman 85 times. On the bad side, cloning would play serious hob with genealogy. A single family group sheet would require a forklift to carry.

Worse, imagine being sealed for time and all eternity to a whole bunch of yourselves.

# Daze of 47: An Hysterical Enactment

MONDAY WAS THE BIG DAY FOR MORMON pioneer enthusiasts. In a reenactment of the 1847 crossing of the plains by the original Mormon pioneers, a wagon train left Winter Quarters, Nebraska, bound for Utah.

According to news reports, the people involved in this venture want the experience to be as realistic as possible. They're using wagons, bonnets, campfire cooking, and even the original Mormon trail when they can.

So accurate is this reenactment that on Monday the new pioneers hadn't gone two miles before getting in trouble with the police for causing traffic jams. As usual, the damn gentiles were mad because the Mormons weren't leaving town fast enough.

I thought about making the 1997 pioneer trek myself for awhile. After all, what better way to gain a deep, abiding appreciation for the faith of your ancestors than to re-enact one of their heroic struggles? Personally, though, I draw the line at staring at an ox's butt for 900 miles.

I decided to stay right here in Utah and re-enact the historical (and occasionally successful) struggle my ancestors made to stay on the good side of Church leaders. Just as it was for Kirbys and Felts 150 years ago, it's a full-time job.

Besides, I've crossed Nebraska and southern Wyoming before in the summer. Even with air conditioning and a CD player it wasn't much fun. I don't even want to think about trying it on foot.

Also, religious re-enactments make me squeamish. They have this disturbing way of getting out of hand. Probably because religious people invariably want to re-enact bad stuff. And the more they want to manifest their faith, the more realistic they want that bad stuff to be, including burnings, floggings, etc.

A prime example of this run amok faith occurred in the Philippines last Easter. According to an Associated Press story, some people there re-enacted the death of Christ by having themselves crucified.

For you historical perfectionists, this annual event is not entirely a symbolic crucifixion. They use real crosses, real nails and real people. The one glaring anachronism being the substitution of a village idiot or two for the Son of God.

Fortunately, Mormons haven't gone to such lengths yet. It could happen though. I know

Mormons extreme enough to re-enact the Carthage Jail martyrdom by volunteering to get shot like Joseph Smith. Not fatally, of course. Maybe just in the leg. You could get a lot of miles out of something like that on the fireside circuit.

As safe as it currently sounds, this Mormon trek stuff could get out of hand too.

Native American tribes along the way might decide they want to make an historical statement of their own. In commemoration of his ancestors' anger over being invaded, a modern Pawnee might take it into his head to pot a couple of Mormons with archery blunts.

Worse, some 1997 pioneer might start thinking that the trip isn't spiritual enough because it lacks real suffering. Chronic dysentery could be reenacted with daily doses of modern laxatives. Stranger things have been known to happen under a prairie sun.

If the trekkers want to simulate the thrill and danger of a buffalo stampede, they could try driving those covered wagons in the eastbound lanes of the interstate. When it comes to a truly "uplifting" experience, nothing beats an 80-mph Freightliner.

Never mind. The important thing here is to remember that it's "historical," not "hysterical."

# UNITED DISORDER

OT LONG AFTER I GOT MY FIRST REAL JOB—
catching rats at Ft. Douglas—I became an
avowed capitalist. Actually, it was that first
glimpse at the amount of money I paid in taxes that
did it.

The money the government took supposedly went
for important programs. All I knew is that I didn't see
any welfare or foreign aid recipients helping me earn
my money. Nope. There in the dark it was just me
and the vermin.

It got worse. Apparently not satisfied with just a
piece of me, Congress tried to draft the rest of me. In
my opinion, both of these things fall under the head-
ings of "robbery" and "slavery." Today, I get real nervous when bureaucrats start feeling magnanimous
with me and mine.

Needless to say, then, that I wouldn't have been a sterling participant in something called the "United Order of Enoch."

In 1874, Brigham Young urged Mormon settlements to start living a communal order wherein everyone gave all their property over to the Church. In turn, the Church gave back only what each person/family needed to live on.

Each person then received a "stewardship" in the form of a community oriented job. At the end of the year, excess profits from these stewardship were blown in a single night of frenzied debauchery. Wait, that isn't it. They were turned over to the Church.

Back then, Mormons lived the United Order in varying degrees. Some didn't live it at all. The idea of working together for the common good wasn't the problem so much as it was deciding on what the common good would be.

Other Mormons got into the Order big time. They formed communes where everyone dressed the same, ate together in large dining halls, and lived in identical houses. An elected board regulated education, entertainment and cooking. Sounds fun, if you like ant farms.

I couldn't have done it. I'm too self-centered. Then again, maybe experience has taught me to be suspicious of group mandated behavior. A common purpose doesn't always mean common sense is involved. If God has tried to teach people anything, it's that when 10 million of us do a stupid thing, it's still a stupid thing.

Right off the top, there's the issue of personal freedom. For example, if the Order decided everyone should wear corduroy pajamas and drink Yoo-Hoo for breakfast, the individual in me wants to be able to tell the group to go to hell without being locked in a pillory for my trouble.

Nor would I want a group choosing my career or stewardship path. If it did, I'd probably still be catching rats or walking circles around an ammo dump somewhere.

Then there's the matter of personal initiative. I wouldn't like working ten times harder than my neighbor Frank only to see Frank making the same amount of money while doing five times the amount of fishing.

Where hard work is concerned, personal starvation is frequently a much better motivator than a

notion of the common good. The federal government ought to try it.

Mercifully, Mormons no longer live the United Order, except maybe when it comes to stuff like academic freedom, R-rated movies and missionary fashion statements. In those particular cases, however, we call it correlation.

# Time and All Eternity

A COUPLE OF WEEKS AGO, I WAS SITTING IN sacrament meeting listening to Brother Rump blather on about the Ten Tribes of Israel when it suddenly occurred to me that I needed some closure in my life.

I went out into the foyer and pulled the fire alarm.

OK, I'm kidding. I was going to pull the alarm but my wife stopped me. She suggested that I offer up my frustration to the Lord as a sacrifice. It was a nice thought. Sacrificing Brother Rump was a better one, though. Apparently he had forgotten that time and all eternity doesn't apply to meetings.

In 40+ years of church attendance, I've had to sit through too many meetings where the speaker rambled on long past the point of common sense. Sometimes full of the Spirit, but more often just full of himself, the person doing the talking carried the meeting beyond the bounds of time and tolerance.

This isn't just a Mormon thing either. I've been to other churches enough to know that while Mormons may claim to be the one and only true faith, we certainly don't have the market cornered when it comes to being windy.

Just because a person is talking in church doesn't mean that he has anything of value to say or that he won't overstay his welcome saying it. Proof is that in some LDS chapels, warning lights are built right into the lecterns. When the speaker sees the light come on, he knows it's time to shut his yap.

The trouble is that the bishop is the only one with

access to the button. The congregation, often because of politeness or lethargy, has to sit there and take it. Of course, some may argue that the Spirit will dictate a flexibility in the length of a sacrament meeting. They're absolutely right.

I would, however, like to point out that if the Spirit can move a speaker to say certain things, why can't it also move him to be succinct and/or even interesting?

The Spirit tells me that there are ways for long-suffering congregations to get closure. Properly executed, future speakers will be horrified at the possibility of them, or a restraining order will bar you from all Church property. Either way, problem solved.

* I already mentioned the fire alarm. A good alternative is a fire hose. Testing on dogs has proved that when it comes to breaking an overly fixed train of thought, nothing works like cold water. Especially 40 cubic feet per second of it.

* A gallon jar of killer bees is sure to pick up the pace of a meeting. And since noise bothers killers bees a lot, microphone feedback from hysterical parishioners is sure to speed things right along.

* There's an old pioneer axiom: The spirit is always on the side of the best marksman. When it comes to getting a dullard's attention, it's hard to beat a pellet gun.

* Crying "snake!" will work, especially if you've actually got some. A couple of handfuls flung into the congregation should do it. Spirit or not, Brother Whackman's 157 reasons why home teaching is important just can't compete with a pit viper.

* Ask questions. As near as I can tell, there's nothing in the rules that says the congregation can't

ask a speaker questions. If Sister Wallop claims that paying tithing makes rubber grow back on car tires, raise your hand and demand proof. It's your right.

WARNING: Don't do any of this stuff because I tell you to. Wait for the Spirit.

# LIGHTMINDED LEGEND

THE HARDEST I EVER LAUGHED IN CHURCH WAS the time my friend Leon Krygowski fell off the podium while passing the sacrament.

It happened because Leon had to wear his older brother's pants to church. I know because I helped Leon ruin his own church pants the day before by daring him to ride his bike off our garage roof.

Anyway, after passing the sacrament to the bishop, Leon had just started down the podium steps when the pants slipped off his skinny hips. Grabbing at them, he missed the first step. This caused him to career down the remainder of the steps and bash headlong into Sister Gwathney with a fully loaded tray of water.

Myself and six other deacons nearly died of heart attacks. We didn't laugh right out loud, of course. We finished our sacred duty blind and red faced. Most of us anyway. On the verge of incontinency, Ralph finally staggered out into the foyer where he collapsed howling.

After church, the bishop herded the Aaronic Priesthood into a room and tore into us about the evils of lightminded behavior. According to him, laughing during the sacrament was right up there with murder, something that we already knew from

last year's Scout camp would keep us from going on missions.

This is one of the problems I have with organized religion. Regular church attendance invariably gives people a clear idea of the things that make God mad enough to kill them, but absolutely no idea what makes him laugh.

Why is that? Maybe it's because a church's purpose is to get us to pay attention to God, and it's easier to do that by scaring the crap out of us than by getting us to lighten up. That's probably why most paintings of God make him look scary enough to cause cancer and why Jesus never smiles in his.

Personally, I think God has a ripping sense of humor. It's people who have weaned religion from the benefits of laughter. We have this moronic tendency to become dangerously self-important about our beliefs, as if God is on our side rather than it being of necessity the other way around.

This general shunning of laughter in religion has contributed to the stereotypical image of devout believers as a bunch of sourpusses whose colons have been tied in knots. We're known for our infatuation with sackcloth, martyrdom and a level of piety that sometimes leads us to social behavior that would embarrass a school of hammerhead sharks.

If laughing about church stuff is a sin, why isn't it a bigger sin to take it too seriously? Sure, laugh too much and you may hurt your ability to be spiritual. Don't laugh enough, however, and you could end up being dangerous to everyone around you. History backs me up here. How many clowns and stand-up comics can you name who have led jihads and pogroms?

According to a recent Associated Press story,

laughter "lowers blood pressure, increases muscle flexion and triggers a flood of beta endorphins." Mirth also increases cells that combat viruses and tumors. Move over Word of Wisdom.

Thirty years later, I can't remember much of what the bishop said about reverence in the chapel. I'm still thanking God for making Leon such a klutz, though. Memory of the sacrament cup stuck behind the dripping lens of Sister Gwathney's cat eye glasses has gotten me through many a dull church meeting.

# Two & a Half Minutes of Eternity

I GAVE MY FIRST TALK IN CHURCH WHEN I WAS
seven. MY mom helped. Standing behind me,
she whispered the words which I then repeated
in a trembling voice to the entire snickering Junior
Sunday School.

To this day, I still associate the smell of a certain
perfume with the nearly uncontrollable urge to go to
the bathroom and/or choke the life out of Wally
Beeder.

Boils, leprosy, demonic possession, of all the bad
things that can happen in connection with religion,
kids know that giving a talk in church is the worst.

Mormons get church talk experience early. Even
before they're out of diapers, we encourage our kids
to get up in front of the congregation and say stuff. If

...AMEN. (Ahem) THE VIEWS EXPRESSED WERE THOSE OF SISTER FINKEL and DO NOT NECESSARILY REFLECT THOSE OF the MANAGEMENT OR THIS FIVE YEAR-OLD.

we're lucky, it'll be the same stuff verbatim that was said by the kid just in front of them. If not, it'll be something that makes your family the butt of ward jokes for weeks to come.

When I was a kid, the worst thing that could happen to me was a toss between liver for dinner or my dog getting hit by a car. Right after that, though, was a thing called (ominous drumroll) the "two-and-a-half minute talk."

It went something like this: On Sunday, you'd be

standing around church like a dork: bow tie, arms folded, hair combed like Ozzie Nelson. An adult would walk up and say the words that made the world go dark. "We want you to give a two-and-a-half minute talk next week."

Monday through Saturday was spent putting the talk out of your mind for the sake of sanity. You didn't mention the talk to anyone until five minutes before church on Sunday, and then only to Mom while she frantically searched the yard for your good shoes.

In those final minutes before church, your nearly homicidal mother whipped together a talk for you on love, patience, kindness, or some other equally improbable subject. Meanwhile,the only spirit you're feeling is the one urging you to barf.

A short time later, blind with fright, you're repeating the talk in Sunday School. If you're lucky, you won't start crying or wet your pants before you finish.

Although adults claimed that Jesus was proud of boys and girls who gave talks, every kid knew that this was less important than how their peers felt about it. After all, it wasn't Jesus on the back row sticking out his tongue and making pig faces at you.

Although Mormon kids still give talks in church, we don't call them two-and-a-half minute talks anymore. Which is too bad. If nothing else, the talks helped teach kids an important gospel principle. When two minutes stretches into two hundred years, you get a better idea of how long damnation lasts.

This early talk experience stands Mormons in good stead later as adults, mainly because the burden of speaking in church never lets up. No matter how old you are, there's always the chance that someone will ask you to give a talk on a given topic. By then, however, you hopefully understand the merits in screwing up.

The last time I agreed to give a talk in church, the preselected subject was "love at home." My talk was titled, "How to love people you'd really rather see dead or in prison." That was in 1987. I haven't been asked since.

# SEX AS A WEAPON

THIS COLUMN IS ABOUT SEX. I'M GIVING FAIR warning because this is Utah, and some people may wish to avert their eyes. Also, because it's quite possible that I don't know everything there is to know about sex. Hey, I'm married.

What I do know about sex I learned mostly from my parents, school, various girlfriends, marriage, Scout camps and assorted covert magazines. Namely, that while sex could make you deliriously happy, it could also get you sent to hell or arrested.

The best lessons came from my best friend Kenny ("So much fun you'll think your brain is melting"), Coach Stevens ("You idiots pay attention or you'll get some girl pregnant") and my wife ("Lock the door.").

My least favorite sex lessons came from church. I have vivid memories of sitting in Sunday School while pinch-faced teachers told everyone exactly what God thought of boys and girls who did nasty things. According to them, having sex outside of marriage was "second only to murder."

If the point was to convince me that sex was sacred, it didn't work. At such a tender age, it merely reinforced something I had long suspected: that it was almost OK to hit girls with rocks rather than let them give me cooties. Also, that God would mash me like a bug if I didn't protect myself.

Which, of course, is nonsense. First of all, cooties are great. Take it from me; once you get cooties for real, you can never get enough.

Second, nobody is going to convince me that a few passionate moments at a drive-in when you're sixteen is anywhere close to murder. Unless, of course, the girl's father catches you.

The worst church lesson about the sanctity of sex didn't happen to me. It happened to one of my daughters during a Young Women's meeting several years ago. In an attempt to convince the girls of the importance of remaining virgins, an instructor passed around a plate of gum. Wait, it gets better.

One of the sticks of gum had already been chewed. The girls were then each invited to take a piece. As expected, no one took the chewed one. The point was that no self-respecting husband would ever want a bride who was chewed gum.

I think this would be a great gospel lesson on chastity if it wasn't a criminally stupid one first. If you don't think so, then we should meet. You need to show me the more important side of this pathetic analogy, the part where repentance unchews the gum. You also need a whack on the head.

See, despite what you may have heard, Brother and Sister Flanders, plenty of sins come closer to murder than sexual transgression: child abuse, wife beating, rape, cheating widows, and rooting for the U, to name just a few.

Using that gum analogy on my daughter comes pretty close to murder, too. If you don't think so, try it again.

Granted, chastity is an important part of being Christian. But it can't be taught effectively by hooking it to a big load of guilt. Making a person feel like something stuck on the bottom of God's shoe isn't what we're supposed to be about.

When it comes to the gospel, understanding and forgiveness can't be achieved through fear and shame. That's because what makes the gospel wonderful is the same thing that makes sex wonderful: love.

# Honky Tonk Heaven

S OMETHING HAPPENED TO ME ABOUT A YEAR AGO that was either a miracle or a bit of damnation. I started listening to country music.

Oh, quit it. Like you've never done something embarrassing.

I made the switch in part because one of my favorite radio stations changed their format from rock to range. Also, one of the station's radio personalities, Dan Bammes, is a friend of mine. He bet me that country music wouldn't give me the bloody flux, a long-held personal belief.

Since then, I've actually acquired a small CD collection of singers like George Strait and Reba McEntire. They're a vast improvement over the country twangers of my youth: Charley Pride, Johnny

Paycheck and Tammy Whine-it, people I previously considered only marginally human.

What troubles me now about country music is that very little of it seems to be coming out of Utah. Hey, if any group of people can be considered unsophisticated, backward and rural, it ought to be Mormons.

So why aren't there more LDS country music stars? Think about it. When it comes to moaning about life's miseries, we should be better than most. If a song about your wife leaving can become a hit, think what a song about eight wives leaving could do. If you think eight seconds on the back of a Brahma bull is tough, try two years in Uruguay.

Some might say that it's because Mormons don't drink, a popular misery theme of many country tunes. Bull. You want real misery, try coping with the fact that your grandma got hit by a train and you can't get drunk to feel better about it. Talk about your agricultural angst.

The same can't be said about rock music and Mormons. Drugs, love-ins, surfing and magic buses aren't our things. Trouble with wives, farms, Missouri, God and the federal government are.

Country music would be a lot different today if it had been heavily influenced by Mormons instead of cowboys. Today, country superstars would be making Utah famous instead of everybody yodeling about how great Texas is, which is a lie. Then again, I've only been to Amarillo.

I'm serious. Imagine a Mormon Tim McGraw hitting the big time singing "Don't ordain the girl," or, "I'm a missionary outlaw, half BYU and Utah—my baby's accidentally a maw-maw." Go ahead, tell me

Mormons wouldn't clean up the Country Music Awards.

Maybe country music would have meant more to me back in the old days if Johnny Paycheck had sang "Take this calling and shove it" or if Charley Pride's hit had been "See an angel in the morning."

Today, Deanna Carter would be singing "Strawberry Kool-aid," instead of "Strawberry Wine." Rhett Akins would be wailing, "If you don't want to hear how the waters parted, don't set me a parted." Meanwhile, Toby Keith is complaining that he "should've been a Catholic."

All aspects of Mormon life would be covered, from excommunicated dissident Billy Dean singing "that church has been spying on me" to the more orthodox Mormon country group Diamond Rio urging people to "fast a little longer."

Then again, maybe it's better that things worked out the way they did. A strong Mormon influence on country music is one thing, a strong country influence on the Tabernacle Choir is another.

No way will I ever be ready for an angelic chorus singing "a ride with me, 'tis eventide."

# MESSING WITH MASS

I'M GOING TO ATTEND CATHOLIC MASS ON Christmas Eve this year. As a Mormon, there's a small chance that God will see me doing this and zap me. On the other hand, I've done worse stuff before and He never hurt me.

Still, it's worth the risk because this is a very special Mass. Serious overcrowding at St. Francis of Assisi in Provo has forced Utah County Catholics to search for a larger building to hold their Mass.

The problem is that all the larger buildings suitable for holding this service belong to the enemy: Mormons. Turns out that it wasn't as big a problem as you might think. So, for the first time ever, Catholics will celebrate their Christmas Mass in the Provo LDS Tabernacle.

At the risk of sounding unspiritual, I'd like to say that it's about damn time.

Just so you know, this is a full-service Catholic Mass, complete with holy water, a crucifix, wine, incense—the works. Better yet, there'll be three of them, starting at 5:30 P.M. and ending at midnight.

Even more surprising is the fact that LDS church officials agreed to it. In a sacred building where men with names like Young, Talmage, Smith and Cannon once thundered the doctrine of God's "one and only true church" to Mormon Saints, Catholics will kneel and pray to their own saints. Is this cool or what?

Everybody knows, of course, that Mormons and Catholics have fundamental religious differences, not the least of which is the football whupping BYU handed Notre Dame two years ago. Lesser differences include stuff like baptizing babies, the sacrament, marriage, etc.

Over the years, these differences have kept Mormons and Catholics polarized, especially in Utah County where a surprising number of Catholics, being Latinos, don't even speak English. What we have then is two groups of people interested in doing good while at the same time blithely ignoring each other.

The ironic part is that we both know better. Anyone who belongs to a religion founded on the tenants of Christianity knows that Jesus never said, "Love thy fellow selves."

The truth is that Mormons and Catholics (or any one else) are not as different as we'd like to think. We've simply gotten dumb about each other by reinforcing what differences do exist to the point where we're no longer able to see our common bonds.

Years ago, I arrested a young Latino male for possession of marijuana. During the booking process, he started to cry. Using my Mormon mission Spanish, I asked him what was wrong. I almost laughed when he said that his arrest would humiliate his parents because they were Catholic.

My first thought was to trivialize his problem because he wasn't even a member of the "true" church. This was, of course, a stupid thought because it arrogantly assumed that disappointing Mormon parents had to be worse than disappointing Catholic parents. After all, God expects less from Catholics, right?

To keep this sort of nonsense from ever occurring to me again, I'm going to Mass on Christmas Eve. It won't change my personal religious beliefs but there's a good chance that it'll improve my view of Catholics and help me regard them as part of my extended family. Frankly, I don't think you could ask for a better Christmas gift.

But just in case my wife is reading, I'd like to point out that I still want a new CD player.

# LOCAL GOD

THE *DESERET NEWS* RECENTLY CHANGED ITS masthead to include the phrase "Utah's locally owned daily newspaper."

The phrase is a subtle dig at rival papers like *The Salt Lake Tribune* which was recently acquired by TCI, a Colorado-based corporation. Also the *Ogden Standard-Examiner*, which was bought by Sandusky Newspapers, Inc., way back in Ohio.

Oh, and let's not forget *The Daily Herald* down in Provo, which was recently gobbled up by the Pulitzer newspaper chain from Missouri.

The meaning, I suppose, is that because it's locally owned the *News* is more in touch with local readers. It's a nice thought even if it isn't entirely an accurate one. Trust me, I've done my research on this. It's very simple.

Fact 1: The *News* is owned by the LDS church.

Fact 2: The LDS church is owned by God.

Fact 3: Mormons believe that God lives on Kolob.

Fact 4: Kolob is way further away from Utah than either Colorado, Missouri, or Ohio.

So, as any idiot can see, the *Tribune* could be owned by somebody living on Mars and still have a better claim to being "locally owned" than the *Deseret News*.

Having thus crushed the opposition's logic by proving beyond a shadow of a doubt that God is an absentee landlord, it's time to move on to more spiritual matters.

Newspapers aren't the only ones who make such ridiculous claims. Churches do it too. In fact, churches do it the most. All of them claim that their faith is locally owned, meaning that God is their homey and nobody else's.

As such, no one can really know God if they aren't from the same barrio. God, as you all know, is very particular about who he hangs with. Throw the wrong kind of sign at God and you're going down, brother.

All of this would make perfect sense if it wasn't perfectly stupid first. God's hood is the entire universe, which makes geography pretty much a moot point. When it comes to caring about people, God doesn't get into pointless turf wars. He's as local as you can get.

The question really is then whether *you're* locally owned. Proof isn't in where you stand but rather what you do. Mormon, Catholic, Jewish or whatever, the purpose of most religions is to make you a better person than the one you're naturally inclined to be. And if you're a jerk, it isn't working.

That isn't God's fault or even (most of the time) the fault of your religion. Ninety-nine percent of the time, it'll be your fault. Either you weren't paying attention or you got off on a rant somehow. Your first clue should have been when you started thinking that God likes you better.

Make all the noise about it that you want, but it all still comes down to performance. Whether it's business, religion, human relations, or even drag racing, the proof of your claims always shows up best in the results. Everything else is just smoke and noise.

For Christians, this is what Jesus was talking about when he said, "Not every one that saith unto me, Lord, Lord, shall enter in the kingdom of heaven; but he that doeth the will of my Father which is in heaven."

For those of you not scripturally inclined, I'll take the liberty of paraphrasing the Savior here.

"Talk is cheap. Let's see what you got."

# AMATEUR HOUR

LAST WEEK, I ATTENDED CHURCH IN SEATTLE, Washington. I might as well have stayed home. It was the exact same service as the one I get in Springville, only wetter and greener.

The Seattle ward followed the meeting script to the letter. They had a prayer, a few announcements, some singing, a couple of long-winded talks, and another prayer. All while kids in the congregation hooted, screeched and bonked their heads on pews. Gripping stuff.

Had we not been visiting friends, I would have gone to the Hallelujah Morning Baptist church down the block instead. Tell the truth, how often do you get a chance to worship and do aerobics at the same time?

## THE CHURCH is the SAME NO MATTER WHERE YOU ARE...

SPRINGVILLE, UTAH        COCHABAMBA, BOLIVIA

But perhaps the biggest difference between my church and other churches is that the clergy in other churches are trained ministers. They get paid (not very much) to be the spiritual guides for a congregation of people who expect them to know the answers to stuff God cares about.

With Mormons, it's a bit tougher. Our preachers are us. Nine times out of ten, we're stuck listening to someone talk in church who may be an expert on welding or pig farming but just so-so when it comes to the Atonement.

Generally speaking, Mormons put the concept of a paid clergy on a par with sacrificing animals. We're proud of the fact that our ward services are run by willing volunteers, earnest amateurs and sometimes even complete dolts.

Whereas other churches have strict guidelines on who gets to shout from the pulpit, Mormons don't. Other churches meticulously search for pulpit fodder. None of this ten years of theology school and a master's degree in sociology for us. The only credentials a person needs to preach in an LDS ward are:

* Be new to the ward
* Be leaving the ward
* Be a BYU football player
* Say yes, no matter how reluctantly

Despite the obvious drawbacks, there's an advantage to this. Not only does the Church save money on preachers, but everyone knows that no matter how bad Brother Fishliptz' talk was, there's the distinct possibility that yours will be even worse. It's humbling.

Another big difference is that a paid clergy is usually professionally trained to handle spiritual and emotional woes. Take something like a spouse abuse problem to an amateur and the prescribed treatment can range anywhere from a gift subscription to a Church magazine to the loan of a handgun.

Frankly, I wish I'd had a little more paid clergy training before I went on my mission. One of my companions certainly needed it. Hey, when the branch president is a 19-year-old virgin from American Fork, a prebaptism interview with a 32-year-old recently reformed prostitute can be a grueling experience.

The downside of a regular minister is that he or she can become predictable. When the same person preaches every Sunday, the entertainment value tends to wane. You know they're going to say something like ". . . and Jesus said unto them, 'Love one another.'"

Not so in my church. When you draw from the audience, you never know what you're going to get. Occasionally, it's something like ". . . and so, brothers and sisters, Jesus obviously likes Utah the best."

Even though I complain about how boring it is, I'd probably miss my own church if I only went to the others. I enjoy the others, but when it comes to entertainment, you really can't beat amateur hour.

# MORMON TORTURE DEVICE

I RECEIVED A LETTER FROM A READER A FEW DAYS A go asking for some spiritual advice. Among other things, the woman from Provo wanted me to help her understand a specific of worship.

"If your [sic] as smart as you think you are," she wrote, "what would you do to make church any better?"

I actually have several projects in the works to help improve the quality of Sunday worship. Whether or not they'll ever come to fruition depends largely on how open-minded local religious leaders are. Which, of course, means that I've got my work cut out for me.

I find it a bit ironic that although we're counseled to seek the truthfulness of the gospel with our hearts, the truth is that we spend a lot of time looking for it with our butts. Meaning that in church we worship a lot sitting down.

While it's probably different in other faiths, Mormons spend an average of about three hours per Sunday on their hams. Some of us, those with intensive Sunday church jobs, spend double that. The burning we get from it has little to do with the spirit.

Which brings us to the seat of the problem, namely where we park our behinds while worshipping. In the Springcreek 8th Ward, about half of us sit on cushioned pews. A quarter of us get padded wooden chairs. The rest, those late or unlucky, get folding chairs in the back.

From personal experience, I can tell you that you don't need a cushioned pew to worship from in order to feel the spirit. I've sat through church services on a variety of seats, including a packing case, a cement floor, a saw horse, a tailgate, and on a few memorable

LDS
TORTURE
DEVICE

occasions, the top of an Army helmet.

Truthfully, when no pews are available, I prefer the helmet to the average LDS ward folding chair, which Bagley describes as "a Mormon torture device second only to a handcart."

Granted, some pews are better than other pews. For sheer proof of your faith, forget cushioned pews. You want a plain wooden pew, one that after three hours makes your butt feel like it went nine rounds behind a wood shed.

Some of this may account for why some people have such a hard time paying attention in church. After all, when your butt has gone to sleep it's a bit hard for the rest of you not to follow suit.

So in an effort to make worship services more bearable if not spiritual, I've come up with something better. I started out with a basic recliner, something that would allow a worshipper to really kick back on those interminable high council Sundays.

Taking a note from movie theaters, a Tupperware holder was installed for kid snack containers. Small speakers are located in the wing backs. I thought about putting a hymnal pouch on the side but changed my mind.

The speakers would allow a worshipper to tune into a recorded conference talk (or even a ball game with the right tinkering) if bored with the current talk. As for the hymnals, I've dumped them in favor of an electronic reader displaying hymn lyrics at the front of the chapel.

Tentatively my new church seat is called the "Lay-Z-Pew," although "Mormo-lounger" is still being considered. It's a revelation in new-age church seating.

And you thought I was just sleeping in church.

# FAMILIES AREN'T FOREVER

ONE OF THE THINGS THAT SETS THE LDS church apart from the other churches is the claim "families are forever." That and eternal marriage.

This means, of course, that if you behave yourself down here, you'll be reunited with your family in the next life.

I used to get a lot of miles out of this eternal family stuff back when I was a missionary. Most people get misty-eyed when they hear that they get to spend eternity with their kids and spouse. They like being together. It's sort of why they got married and had a family in the first place.

That was when I was a missionary. I've been a dad for 20 years now and long ago came to the conclusion that "families are forever" is less of a promise from

God than it is a warning. Maybe even a curse.

I don't know about you, but the last thing I want when it comes to a heavenly reward is to spend eternity or even a few trillion years stuck in a car with a bunch of diapered trolls who want to know if we're "there yet."

I think some people go for this idyllic family stuff because it's romantic. It probably tugs at their heart. They think it's going to be the Waltons in white, just them and little Jeffy bouncing a ball, eating family dinners and going for walks in heaven. I don't think so.

In the first place, they aren't your kids, they're God's kids—and, incidentally, so are you. That makes you and your kids brothers and sisters. Equals. You aren't going to be the mom and dad of anyone. God is.

So, if your kids are jerks now when you're in

FAMILIES
✲ ARE ✲
FOREVER

charge, just imagine how it's going to be when you're equals. Try telling them they can't stay out late then.

The fact that my kids and I will be equals in heaven doesn't bother me. In fact, I actually like the idea because (a) I won't have to support them and (b) nobody can sue me for what they do.

Better yet, I'm betting that knocking your brother unconscious in heaven, like on earth, is less of a bad thing than it would be if he's your smart-ass kid. Say, oh, the difference between a felony sin and a misdemeanor peccadillo.

In the second place, not only will some people not want to be the mom and dad in heaven, they aren't going to want to be the husband or wife either. They just spent 50+ years in a marriage that was hell. Why in heaven's name would they want it to keep going forever?

Personally, I'm looking forward to being with my wife forever. I like her a lot. That's why we got married. We also wanted a family. Back then, we were too young to know that there's nothing quite like a kid with a stubbed toe howling at your locked bedroom door to make you wish you'd been born sterile instead.

No matter what they say in church, kids drive parents apart. If you don't think so, take a look at the families in church next time. The more kids a family has, the further apart mom and dad have to sit. Maybe that's why there's no mention of a mother in heaven.

OK, I'm not saying that families aren't forever, only that in heaven families aren't going to be anything like they are down here. Praise the Lord.

# BISHOP-WRECK

O N THE SURFACE, THE BISHOP OF AN LDS ward seems a rather powerful man. Within the confines of a ward, the bishop's got the ultimate say on how funds get dispersed, which activities are held, and who gets whacked with a calling or a court.

The only time you actually need to worry about this ecclesiastical power is if you actually attend a ward. Church-going Mormons know full well that a bishop can greatly bless or distress their lives.

But even if you aren't a Mormon, this is still Utah and that means you technically live within the boundaries of a Mormon ward. It's therefore a good idea to know who the boss Mormon is. The bishop's phone number belongs right there next to the emergency numbers for police, fire, and poison control.

If the missionaries start wearing a path in your lawn, or Mormon kids become more unruly than usual, you'll know who to contact for best results. As

# the BISHOP

a rule, Mormons tend to be more scared of our bishops than we are of the police or even the U.S. Army.

Despite how it sounds, a bishop isn't all powerful. Or at least he's not supposed to be. A bishop is actually part of something called a "bishopric," a four-man operation more similar to a military junta than an actual dictatorship.

In addition to the bishop, a bishopric is comprised of two counselors and a secretary. It's their job to try and make the ward run smoothly. They do this mainly by paying close attention to what their wives and Church leaders have to say.

As a kid, I had a hard time with the concept of "bishopric." If our bishop's name was Ed, who the hell was Bishop Rick and why was everyone so worried about what he thought?

Later, I came to understand that "bishopric" wasn't

Bishop Rick but rather "bishop-wreck." This occurred about the time I got old enough to start holding church callings, which invariably conflicted with more pressing things in my life. It's hard to teach Sunday School if you get thrown in jail Saturday night.

Most of a bishopric's time is taken up trying to find people willing to accept church jobs. Although heavenly inspiration is supposed to play a big part in this process, mindless desperation often plays a bigger part.

The last time a bishop claimed he was inspired to call me as ward Scoutmaster, I agreed with him. The big question, however, was whether the inspiration came from God or Satan. He relented when I said the same spirit just might inspire me to use the Scouts as shark chum on our very first outing.

The bishop's two counselors serve as his point men. A truly inspired bishop knows that if the chances of getting assaulted simply by asking someone to be the Primary president are high, it's best to send a counselor. There's two of them and you can always get more.

The bishop's secretary is the ward's sergeant major. Not technically a ward officer, the secretary still has more clout than other enlisted Mormons. A smart bishop uses his secretary to do clerical work and things bishops shouldn't do. Like yanking unruly deacons sideways.

Although a bishopric has a lot of power within a ward, it's been my experience that it rarely gets abused. Given the nature and temperament of the average Mormon ward, most of the power a bishop has is used in self-defense.

# GOING HOME EARLY

ABOUT TWENTY YEARS AGO, MY FRIEND ELLIOT was riding his motorcycle when he ran into the back of a car at a stop light.

The speed of the impact wasn't much, about ten mph, but still fast enough to pop Elliot over the handlebars and into the car's bumper. He was DOA at University Hospital.

Elliot's death devastated his circle of friends. We all asked ourselves why? Being a band of hopeless pagans, none of us had any real answers.

Several speakers at Elliot's funeral claimed to have the answer. They said that God took Elliot because he needed him in heaven for a special mission. It was a nice answer and made everyone feel better if not exactly smarter.

Twenty years later, I still don't buy it. My bet is

that God didn't TAKE Elliot to heaven as much as he LET Elliot come. I think my friend got killed because he wasn't paying attention or wearing a helmet.

At least part of my basis for this belief is the popular Mormon notion that God operates on a different time level than the rest of us—the general theory being that a thousand years on earth is roughly equivalent to a day in heaven.

If this is true, can anyone tell me what was so all-fired important that God couldn't wait five seconds for Elliot to die of old age instead of whacking him with a Ford? You'd think that God would be better organized than that.

Seeing God's hand in untimely deaths is a way of sparing ourselves from the cold reality that stuff like this usually just happens. And the dumber you are, the better the odds are that it will happen to you.

The flip side of this God/death question is the sole survivor issue. You see it a lot in the news: Fred wanders out of a plane crash that killed his 250 fellow passengers. When the news focuses on Fred's family, they're all tearfully grateful that God spared him. To pay God back, Fred promises to become a priest or at least stop drinking so much.

What's never said in situations like this is why God liked Fred better than the other 250 people who got cooked? What was so special about a portly insurance agent that he lived while three dozen children, a concert pianist, two brilliant cancer researchers and six Mary Knollers got fried?

Probably nothing more than the right seat assignment.

Just once, I'd like to see one of these survivors seriously consider the possibility that they lived because God didn't like them. Think about it. Given a choice, what would you rather do: walk the paths of heaven as an angel or sit through a press conference knowing that everyone else on the plane was happy while you still had an inevitable date with cancer or a heart attack to look forward to?

As a Mormon, I hold with the belief that life is nothing more than a temporary state wherein I'm supposed to learn something. Frankly, the pragmatist in me would never stop wondering if being spared wasn't really God making me stay after school because I was such a slow learner.

When it's all said and done, I think God cares less about when and how we die than he does about why and how we lived. As such, the only explanation necessary for death is how prepared you are to meet it.

# Matter Over Mind

ACCORDING TO THOSE IN THE KNOW, GOD ONLY hangs with people whose thoughts are pure. If you want to stay close to God, you have to keep your mind clean; if not completely and totally hygienic, at least dusted off.

Back when I was a missionary, I had a hard time keeping my thoughts pure. Actually, I wasn't even trying to reach pure. I would have settled for "slightly soiled" or even "hard to get ground-in dirt." Anything other than the nuclear level filth I was accustomed to would have been an improvement.

My companion at the time, a veteran elder, and therefore older and wiser to the ways of the world than myself, said that the best way to banish carnal thoughts was to sing a hymn. No way, Elder Widge claimed, could Satan stick around through all four verses of "Israel, Israel, God Is Calling."

Unfortunately, I wasn't dealing with just the devil. If I had been, at least it would have been a fair fight. There were also Charlie's Angels, Miss October, Sally Field, Susan Anton, Cinderella, and Sister Jones to consider.

Since Elder Widge never sang hymns to himself, I blithely assumed that he had used the hymn process to become complete master of his thoughts. This was early on in our relationship, before I discovered that Widge had the mental prowess of a mollusk. What's the point of being the master of your thoughts if they can't really take you anywhere?

Anyway, I gave the "will sing for purity" a whirl. It helped at first. "More Holiness Give Me" simply wasn't the sort of background music conducive to a mental romp with Susan Anton and the Bionic Woman.

Unfortunately, I was twenty-one years old and, according to various studies and reports which are not part of the LDS Standard Works, at my sexual peak. As such, the humming of hymns eventually became a nonstop operetta. You've heard of the Singing Nun? Well, I was the Howling Missionary.

I should point out that this process would probably work for other people, those with more manageable and constructive minds. It didn't work for me because my brain is stubborn, not real bright and my worst enemy.

As it turned out, I sang hymns so often that they eventually became a source of erotica to me. By the time Elder Widge got transferred, there wasn't a hymn I could sing without it conjuring the image of Linda Ronstadt wearing nothing but a smile and a pair of cowboy boots. A few bars of "A Poor

"CODE RED—I WANT A DIRECT FEED to HYMN # 187"

Wayfaring Man of Grief" and—poof!—there she was, singing right along.

Needless to say I stopped singing hymns. I tried other things, stuff that wouldn't ruin hymns for me. For a time, I whacked myself in the head whenever a bad thought occurred to me. But after a couple of days it became apparent that if I kept punching myself every time such a situation arose, I would soon beat myself to death.

I also tried cold showers. They didn't work because cold showers were all we had there in Nalgas de Vaca and therefore really not effective as a mental deterrent. If continued, I would have grown gills.

It was the mission president who solved the problem. He sent me to work in a beach town at the peak of the summer season. Within a few days, sensory overload had accomplished what nothing else could. Hey, when you've seen four million girls in bikinis, you've seen them all.

The experience scarred me spiritually though. To this very day, singing in church will sometimes actually get me in the mood.

# "CULT"IVATING A TESTIMONY

WHILE BACK, NEWSWEEK PUBLISHED A LIST OF rules that the Heaven's Gate cult required its members to live by. The rules are so strict that they're a good indication as to why the cultists eventually got weird enough to kill themselves.

I wouldn't have lasted five minutes in Heaven's Gate. The grooming standards alone, which apparently included a very aggressive circumcision policy, would have sent my testimony screaming into the night.

Truth is, I'm probably not geared for religious regimentation of any kind. The fact that the HG list contains a surprising number of things expected out of me by my own church no doubt explains why I'm not your typical goose-stepping Mormon either. Or so I'm reminded about 500 times a week.

When it comes to marching orders, organized religion is worse than the Army. Uncle Sam only wants you to be all that you can be. Religion, on the other hand, wants you to be all that someone else want you to be.

It wouldn't be so bad if that someone else was just God. Unfortunately the list also includes bishops, stake presidents, the Relief Society, elder's quorum, young men's presidents, the building janitor and anyone else with an overly-fixed idea of God's plan for you.

This no doubt explains why the Ten Commandments of old have today become ten thousand rules, policies, guidelines, and directives. Most of which aren't intended to improve your lot in life as much as they're intended to control it.

For example, lack of zealous obedience is high on the list of Heaven's Gate rules just as it is to the thinking of some overly zealous Mormons.

Major Heaven's Gate offenses consisted of violating the chain of command, to wit: lying to leaders, sensual thoughts, not confessing sins to leaders, and deliberately breaking rules.

Both to Heaven's Gate and my bishop, I plead guilty on all charges. Furthermore, I feel real bad that I'm not sorry about it.

Lesser offenses are, as you might expect, more numerous. In an effort to maintain control, Heaven's Gate folks were not supposed to take any action without consulting their "check partner," a person whose job it was to make sure they stayed in line.

Ironically, Mormons aren't either. I've had a variety of check partners throughout my life: my mom, assorted missionary companions, dorm parents, home teachers, and a wife. Although I probably should, I don't count the police.

Criticizing or finding fault with classmates or teachers was a Heaven's Gate no-no. In Mormonese, this is known as speaking ill of the Lord's anointed. Ditto arguing with BYU standards, cheering for the U, or sassing your bishop.

Picking or choosing certain tasks was a bad thing in Heaven's Gate, the logic being that the leaders knew what was best for you. For Mormons, this comes under the heading of never saying no to a church calling. Somewhere we've gotten the idea that whatever a leader wants is automatically what God wants.

Trusting your own mind or your own judgment was also a lesser HG offense. It's a lesser offense for Mormons, too, but only so long as personal revelation doesn't run contrary to church revelation or even correlation.

For example, if the Sunday School Manual says it's time for Lesson #81 "Keeping the Food Storage Holy," and the spirit tells you the lesson is a crock, you aren't supposed to think up a better one on your own.

Also, Heaven's Gate members weren't supposed to have inappropriate curiosities, whatever the heck that means. For Mormons, it means reading *Sunstone*, going to R-rated movies, perusing the *Sports Illustrated* swimsuit edition, and becoming a Democrat.

Being too aggressive or pushy was bad for an HG person. It's also bad for an LDS person unless said person is operating within his official priesthood capacity, be it stake president, bishop, seminary teacher, or simple Danite. Mormons call it "unright-eous dominion."

"Vibrating or expressing masculinity or feminin-ity" in any way is on the list. For Heaven's Gate this apparently referred to hair-dos, makeup and external forms of genitalia. For Mormons, it centers around earrings, specifically which gender can wear them at BYU.

Punishment for breaking any of these lesser offenses in not spelled out by either Heaven's Gate or the LDS church. Maybe that's because overly strict and brainless obedience in either case inevitably becomes its own punishment.

None of this means that the Church is a cult like Heaven's Gate. A lot depends on your personal brand of zealotry. After all, with just the right amount of blind obedience and narrow thinking, a person could make a cult out of any organization.

# The Spirit Slammer

MORMON DOCTRINE CLAIMS THAT WHEN WE die, our spirits go to a place known as the Spirit Prison. There we wait with our lawyers until the great Judgment Day. Animal spirits go to the Spirit Pound.

I've got a problem with the Spirit Prison. Not the place itself, but rather who thought up the name? When I was a missionary, some people I taught got hung up on the Spirit Prison, mistaking it for some degree of hell.

Senor Gomez: "I see. Bad spirits go to prison."

Me: "No. Everyone goes to the Spirit Prison."

Senor Gomez: "Ah, we are all bad spirits then."

Me: "Not everyone. I told you—."

Senor Gomez: "Has anyone ever gone over the wall in this prison? Are there dogs?"

If, as the doctrine claims, the Spirit Prison is a place where the gospel gets preached to those who didn't have a chance to hear it on earth, why call it a prison? After all, nobody's been charged with anything yet. If the U.S. Constitution really is an inspired document, then shouldn't even God need probable cause before slinging people into the slammer?

Maybe it was all the years I spent as a cop. It's just that when someone says prison, I think of a not very nice place to be. Specifically, a place where the chances of getting taught the gospel take a distant back seat to the distinct possibility of getting shanked.

It's probably just semantics. Maybe even anti-semantics. Anti-Nephi-semanti?

Where was I? Oh, yeah, semantics. It's safe to say

DOING HARD TIME in SPIRIT PRISON

that Mormon terminology changes from time to time. We use one phrase until it becomes onerous and then we switch to another.

Remember back when "less active" members were "inactive" members? Or even further back when less active members were "apostates?" Better yet, when "apostates" were "worm food" thanks to Porter Rockwell & Co.

How about when nonmembers were "gentiles" and "this great country" was "Babylon?"

Over the years, the Church changed those names to avoid stigmatizing people (and getting sued into the next millennium). It's a political rather than spiritual move, one that requires careful thought lest you rob a word of it's true meaning.

For example, the word "inactive" brings a brainless couch potato to mind for most of the world. "Inactive" certainly isn't connotative of someone more inclined to spend Sunday on water skis than a folding chair.

So why not soften the blow on this Spirit Prison stuff too? Why not call it the "Spirit Foyer?" I mean when it comes to a waiting room environment, the word "prison" just doesn't get it. It certainly wouldn't raise my morale over what comes next. Maybe that's why nobody refers to the ward house foyer as the "Testimony Jail."

Better yet, call it the "Spirit Lounge." Serve hor d'ouerves and club soda. Muzak.

If the Church wants to stick with Spirit Prison, why not call the testimonies received there "spirit bail?" Why isn't Jesus the "prosecutor" instead of "Savior?" Who's the "spirit bailiff?"

This gospel doctrine stuff sure is tough when you're an idiot breaking new ground.

# PRIVATE INVESTIGATORS

I 'VE GOT THIS NERVOUS FEELING THAT MY WIFE AND I have been targeted for conversion. Mercifully, we're already Mormon and so the feeling doesn't stem from the fact that two kids in suits keep ringing our doorbell.

Having been a full-time missionary myself, I recognize the signs of being targeted. Most common are a sudden interest in your well-being, a desire to become better friends through baked goods, and the occasional non sequitur like, "I know what you mean about aluminum siding, Gus, but do you think Pamela Anderson ever prays about baptism for the remission of her sins?"

Being on the receiving end of this kind of behavior is nothing new for non-Mormons in Utah. They can't go anywhere in this state (except Park City) without three-quarters of the town regarding them as a golden opportunity. It's like living in a state populated entirely by door-to-door salespeople.

But it can happen, even to Mormons. Right here in Zion, I've been targeted for conversion by Jehovah's Witnesses, Seventh Day Adventists, Reorganized Mormons and even a group of fundamentalists who've somehow got repentance confused with rifles. Yet I've managed to stay Mormon.

This time, however, the conversion feeling is coming from a friend who belongs to another church. And even though we hang out together, they still think Mormons are okay. Why just the other day, they told us that they're "pretty sure" Mormons don't drink blood.

It's logical to want to bring your friends around to

your way of thinking. This is especially true with respect to religion where, if you don't, said friends just might go to hell. Trying to convert friends is also easier because friends rarely force you off their property at gunpoint just for bringing up the subject.

Generally speaking, potential converts have to want to be converted in the first place. This happens either because they're interested in what you've got or dissatisfied with what they've got. In gospel parlance, this is known as a "softening of the heart."

God softens people's hearts in a lot of different ways, most commonly via a thoroughly miserable experience that results in a good feeling if not a happy ending. See Job, Jonah, Paul, etc. This method sounds complicated, but then He's God.

People aren't that sophisticated. Historically speaking, people have relied on just two things to soften other people's hearts: friendship or an axe. Simply put, anyone who refused to prove their friendship by converting, we killed.

The modern equivalent of the gospel axe, of course, is to vilify, ostracize and then ignore people who refuse to come around to our way of thinking. Oddly enough, few friends and fewer converts are the result.

There's potential for trouble, however, if the only reason you want to be friends with someone is because you want to convert them. Not only is this shamefully transparent (and typically Utah Mormon), but it is also probably not what God was thinking when he commanded us to "love one another."

Whereas it's understandable to want to share with your friends that which makes you happy, you have to ask yourself if you'll still be friends when and if they say no. If not, then you probably weren't a real friend in the first place, certainly not in the "love one another" category.

The irony here is that in order to convert someone through friendship, you first have to be a friend. Which means you have to convert yourself first.

# PRIESTESSHOOD

ANOTHER LDS GENERAL "CON-FURNZ" HAS come and gone without a revelation concerning Mormon women and the priesthood. Maybe this means the emancipation fervor among some Mormon women is dying out. I hope so because I really don't want them to get the priesthood.

I'll wait until you get done tearing your hair.

OK, the truth is that I don't really care about women and the priesthood. It's God's business and, the last time I checked, He didn't care what I thought.

What bothers me the most about Mormon women holding the priesthood is the fact that having the priesthood is a prerequisite to becoming any kind of Mormon church boss. Frankly, the workings of the Mormon church are already more complicated than DNA. It would be ten times worse if the women had more say.

Calm down. I have proof.

When God created us, he balanced Man's "so what" attitude with Woman's "just so" nature. As

such, women are good at making stuff out of nothing whereas men are good at making nothing out of stuff. We're both happy doing this.

For example, consider the areas set aside for the two genders in an average Utah Mormon ward house. The women meet in the Relief Society room while the men meet in either a closet or the furnace room, whichever happens to be free.

The Relief Society room has cushioned chairs, a piano, a lectern, flowers, and curtains, frills that have become near gospel ordinances to women. The Spirit simply can't be felt in a lesson if the instructor doesn't have a doily to put her chalk and eraser on.

Conversely, the priesthood quorums meet in a room with metal folding chairs, bare windows and no piano. We don't care. For us, it's considered a good day if anyone in the room can remember who's supposed to teach the lesson.

The same disparity exists when it comes to meetings. When Mormon women want to hold a meeting, it requires posters and clever invitations hand-delivered to the homes of all involved. Women stress out if a sister wasn't notified right up to the last minute.

Meetings for Mormon men are conducted on a much simpler level. Technically speaking, a meeting is considered held if at least two people remember to show up, both of whom arrived hoping that no one else would.

In the foyer of the ward house, the Relief Society sets up a table to display crafts and foods featured in the upcoming Home Making Meeting. A lot of work goes into this table. More work, in fact, than Mormon men typically put into an upcoming 50-mile Scout hike.

On a more individual level, consider how much folderol is required for a woman to get ready for church; at least an hour for the hair alone. If it's this bad for a regularly scheduled church meeting, no wonder God keeps the time of the Second Coming a secret.

Men. What can I say? We could show up with our pajama tops tucked into our Sunday pants and think nothing of it. Or we could if it weren't for the fuss women would make.

Do you see what I'm getting at here? Put women in charge of the LDS church and things would get so complicated that only women would have the temperament (or even the inclination) to run them.

There's a bright side. Maybe then men could stay home.

# MISSION BLUES

I'D LIKE TO ASK A PERSONAL FAVOR FROM ALL NON-Mormons. The next time the missionaries show up at your door, be nice to them. You don't have to convert, just don't be rude. Mission life is tough enough without you adding to it.

I also want you to be nice because my parents are thinking about going on a mission. Neither of them have been before and so I've been telling them what hardships to expect in the mission field. And believe it or not, none of them are you.

"The worst part about a mission is being stuck with a companion 24-hours a day," I told them. "It'll always be someone so weird that you'll almost stop believing in God."

"Oh, I'm not worried about that," Dad replied. "Your mother and I will be companions."

"That's exactly what I'm talking about," I said.

Back when I received my mission call, I held with the popular Mormon belief that said call and everything related to it came directly from God.

For Mormon missionaries, this belief is imperative. It's better than having to cope with the only other alternative—that you've been left to survive by your meager nineteen-year-old wits in some loony place where even the CIA won't go anymore.

Today, I still believe that God oversees all. The difference being that since my mission what might have once been interpreted as the behavior of a control freak I now believe is divine proof of a very wry sense of humor.

Nowhere is this more evident than in the assignment of missionary companions. A Mormon missionary serves wherever and with whomever the Church sends. The unspoken gospel principle at work here is obedience—or, more specifically, that Al Unser would sooner ask a monkey to take the wheel than God would take into account your thoughts and feelings on the matter.

I served with 12 companions on my mission. Two were normal, while one was actually a blast. The other nine were various combinations of Richard Simmons and J. Edgar Hoover, guys so insufferable that I sometimes tied myself in bed at night so that I wouldn't get up and choke them in my sleep.

Bullets, floods, lightning, starvation, naked village girls—nothing frets a Mormon missionary as much as a new companion. That's because the mission rules require that the two of you become Siamese twins. You're supposed to eat, sleep, work, pray and get napalm-like diarrhea within arm's reach of each other.

The theory here is that two missionaries will watch each other and help keep each other out of trouble, for which the Lord will bless them with success and joy.

They'll grow in mutual love and respect and eventually become General Authorities. Or possibly not.

From personal experience, I can tell you that being stuck in a place where the only other English-speaking person is a guy who won't wash his feet, hums show tunes and quotes entire chapters of Isaiah always causes more trouble than it prevents.

Living cheek and jowl like that isn't natural behavior even for two people in romantic love, never mind two people who have nothing in common other than the fact that they're both carbon-based life forms.

So be nice to the missionaries. Anyone who can live like that for two years without bloodshed deserves a certain amount of respect regardless of their religious persuasion.

# MAIL CALL

SAW MY PARENTS OFF ON AN LDS MISSION TO Guatemala two weeks ago. Haven't heard from them since. I'm not worried though. Having been on a foreign mission myself, I know that it takes longer to get fourth-class mail from south of the border than it does from Mars.

When I was a missionary, it was a rule that I had to write home once a week. While I stretched, bent or broke most other mission rules, this one I kept faithfully. Not because I feared or respected the mission president, but rather because I wouldn't get any mail back if I didn't.

Mail from home is important to a Mormon missionary, particularly missionaries in places where rats and hookworms rank among the top national products. Missionaries in these places desperately want to know that someone still cares about them. Even better, they want to know who won the Super bowl.

In Uruguay, we received our mail once a week. It came in a package from the mission home every Sunday night. According to some gospel sadist (who I would still love to meet), we technically couldn't open the package until Monday morning, which was prep day and therefore fit to sully with unspiritual news from home.

Alas, there in the small town of San Lugar Horrifico, a huge difference existed between "couldn't" and "shouldn't." Our package frequently fell to the floor in such a way that it was torn to pieces and the mail scattered all over our desks.

Say what you want about other mission experiences, mail from home ranks among the top. Among Mormons far from home, it's guaranteed to lift spirits, heal the sick, and raise the dead.

That's probably why, even though I haven't heard from my folks, I keep writing to them.

Being an older missionary couple instead of the typical idiot elder companionship, there are some mission experiences Mom and Dad simply won't get unless it's from me.

For example, mail that Mormon missionaries do not like to get, but usually end up getting nonetheless, are Dear John letters. Hey, it's a little hard to get yourself up to save souls for God when God can't seem to bother saving your girlfriend for you.

When it comes to the popularity of mail, DJ mail ranks right up there with draft notices, overdrawn bank statements, and letters from twisted friends containing pages torn from the recent *Sports Illustrated* swimsuit edition.

Most of my companions got Dear Johned. At the beginning of their missions, the weekly package contained, on average, nine letters from their one and only, most covered with teddy bear stickers and scripture quotes.

Within a few months, this correspondence had dwindled to one a week. After a year, my companions were lucky to get one a month, sans stickers. The infamous Dear John was preceded by one or two hastily scrawled notes along with photo copies of faith promoting stories from the *Ensign*.

The actual Dear John didn't have to begin with

"Dear Elder . . . " On at least two occasions, it came in the form of a wedding announcement. Yet another occurred when one of my companions got a letter from a former companion of his who had eloped with my companion's girlfriend, a matter unofficially referred to as "mission incest."

For me, it comes down to figuring out a spiritual way of telling my parents that I've sold their motor home and bought some jet skis.

# UTAH MORMON OLYMPICS

AT A PREDOMINANTLY NON-MORMON SOCIAL gathering in Salt Lake on Wednesday night, someone asked me how Mormons felt about the Olympics coming to Utah. My answer was a deep theological examination of the issues surrounding the primary reason why I didn't know.

My best guess is that the coming 2002 Winter Olympic games make most Mormons nervous. This kind of thing has happened to us before. First during the California gold rush, which was quickly followed by the invasion of Johnston's Army, the coming of the railroad and the building of ski resorts.

The Olympics aren't going to be any different. Once again, thousands of strange people with designs on our land, laws and women are going to descend on Zion. Our beliefs will be mocked, our faith ridiculed and our hierarchy substantially enriched. No wonder we're skittish.

There's another reason. Utah Mormons are still recovering from the disheartening revelation earlier this year that while most Utahns are Mormons, most Mormons are no longer American.

Some Mormons fear that the 2002 Winter Olympics will only make this worse. It's going to be harder for us adjust to the idea that, for a time at

least, most people in Utah not only won't be Mormon, they won't be American either. I'm telling you, it's a sign of the times. Get ready for the end.

Hold on. The truth is that Mormons will cope with the next gentile invasion the way we always have. We'll convert some and then jack the prices on everything through the roof for the rest. Question our Christianity if you will, but never ever doubt the Mormon commitment to capitalism.

There may also be hidden advantages to the 2002 games. Lots of other cultures have contributed to make the Olympic games what they are today, why can't we? Curling, skiing, the luge, soccer, none of these were original Greek sports, either.

Short of Steve Young, what better missionary tool could Mormons have than an Olympic sport that is universally recognized as Mormon? We could even get sponsors that reflect Mormon standards. Move over Coca-Cola, here come Kool-Aid, Huggies, and the Wheat Growers of America.

As a monitor and commentator of Mormon's trends and ways, I've got a few event suggestions.

* 1,500 Meter Handcart Dash—Name me an Olympic sport that requires an athlete to drag a cart filled with household furniture and kids up a mountain. As a sport, it makes more sense than bowling.

* Diaper Decathlon—How many diapers can you change in five minutes? Mormon women would understandably dominate this event early on, or at least until feminism makes greater inroads into the LDS church.

* Synchronized Worshipping—Forget synchronized swimming. When it comes to doing things together, by the numbers and without question, you

can't beat a Mormon ward. The gold would stay in Provo for at least the first fifty years.

   * Marathon Mob Chase—It's one thing to be fast on your feet when nobody is chasing you. How much faster would you be if someone was? My bet is that the average 100-pound Mormon missionary can beat anything coming out of Kenya these days.

   * Scripture Chase—For years, time-killing Seminary games have been preparing Mormons for this event. It's time to take it on the road. Get from Isaiah 21:4 to Thessalonians 8:11 in record time and come away with the gold. But no fair hiring someone to break your opponent's knuckles.

# Mormon Costumes

AN ALERT READER SENT ME A LETTER THAT circulated her neighborhood a few days ago. Written by "a few concerned LDS mothers," the letter asked everyone not to let their children dress up like vampires, ghouls, witches and spooks for Halloween.

The gist of the letter was that dressing up like the undead was detrimental to the brains of small children. Among other things, it conveyed to them a false sense of legitimacy when it came to stuff like blood sucking and broom riding.

The letter further suggested that children be encouraged to dress like more upbeat characters; to wit: "clowns, cuddly animals, princesses and cowboys." This will, the letter claims, "encourage children to stay far from a collision with evil and grow closer to Heavenly Father during a celebration that is based on paganism." What a scream.

This letter couldn't have come at a better time— namely now that I'm too old to go trick or treating. Had it come when I was much younger, my friends and I would have gone around to these ladies' houses on Halloween and shown them what happens when high-mindedness collides with a five-gallon bucket of carpet glue.

Seriously, it takes a pretty big stretch of the imagination to believe that traditional Halloween costumes necessarily encourage kids to the dark side. If true, then why wouldn't dressing them up as clowns and animals alternately make them more silly or less housebroken?

Frankly, a kid raised by someone who keeps him in an emotional straightjacket stands a better chance of becoming a career criminal than some kid who dresses up as a vampire or a devil once a year.

But then I could be wrong. For the sake of argument, let's say that dressing up like Freddy Krueger means you'll grow disturbed and confused. Rather than risk it, why not encourage your kids to dress up in more faith-promoting ways?

For the sake of our kids, I've put together a list of Mormon church costumes for next year. Don't get your hopes too high, though. If you think Dracula or Frankenstein are scary, wait 'til you get a load of these.

* Church Correlation Committee Member— Strike fear into the hearts of entire Mormon neighborhoods by going door-to-door on Halloween insisting that everyone act in harmony by passing out the exact same treat.

* Danite—Costume consists of a Book of Mormon and a hood. Announce yourself with the blood-curdling cry, "Trick or blood atonement."

* Seminary Teacher—A white shirt and an earnest look. At each home, insist that the residents bear their testimonies rather than give you some Smarties.

* Polygamist Wife—Long dress with a pillow stuffed under it. During inclement weather, consider renting a pair of plastic bare feet.

* Nauvoo Legion Soldier—Thump on the doors with toy muskets. Even if you get a treat, trash the

place looking for copies of the *Nauvoo Expositor* or *Rolling Stone*.

* Nephi—If someone refuses to give you a treat, don't soap their windows. Instead, smite off their head and kidnap their pet.

* Home/Visiting Teacher—Wait until five minutes before November 1 and then pound on doors shouting "trick or teach!"

* Ward Basketball Player—Throw elbows and taunts while dressed in a sweat-soaked T-shirt. Far more frightening than any goblin.

There's a drawback to these costumes as well. After dressing up like this for a few Halloweens, your kids might not want to do it for real when they grow up.

# SPACE-SHUL SPIRITS

RIGHT NOW I'M THINKING THAT OGDEN *Standard-Examiner* cartoonist Cal Grondahl is a prophet. Not THE prophet, mind you, but certainly A prophet.

Years ago, Cal published a book containing cartoons of earth Mormons trying to cope with space Mormons. Good stuff. My favorite was an earth Mormon and an alien Mormon arguing the important gospel doctrine concept of "flesh and blood" or "slime and scales."

The reason I think Grondahl is a prophet is that his cartoons could be closer to the mark than anyone previously thought, including four out of five LDS general authorities who think he's a dangerous nut.

Scientists recently uncovered a meteorite that

supposedly came from Mars. I say supposedly because there's no return address on the rock.

What the meteorite does have is teensy life forms crawling around on it. Some scientists say the bugs or critters also come from Mars and represent the first concrete evidence of extra-terrestrial life. Other scientists say they don't think so.

It should come as no surprise to religious leader that we are not alone in the universe. We already believe that God is out there somewhere. Why not other forms of life?

If I was the leader of a major religion—say the president of the Mormon church—this space bug stuff would put a serious wrinkle in our future plans.

Just like the recent transition wherein most Mormons now live outside the U.S., it could be possible someday that the majority of Mormons lived in outer space. Things might get a little rocky.

For example, how hard would it be for the Church's correlation committee to come up with a Relief Society lesson on keeping love strong in a marriage if, in the future, 34 percent of all Mormons reproduce by fission?

Also, how would the Church's dress code handle slime, feelers and X-ray vision? BYU might not be such a safe place for earth Mormons to spawn in the future. On the other hand, wouldn't it be great if the Cougars could recruit some Klingons?

Some people think I'm being ridiculous. Space creatures can't be Mormons, they say. Only humans can be Mormons.

That's because heretofore, Mormonism has been an earth religion, and humans are the top form of intelligent life on this planet. You almost never see rabbits trying to convince pigs about the truthfulness of being an herbivore.

But what about the top forms of intelligent life on other planets?

The criteria for converting people to Mormonism today is simple: No matter how weird a group of humans might be, it's still divided into two distinct groups—(a) those who can have the priesthood and (b) those who can't.

It's something else to call a 19-year-old kid from Vernal to the Phobos-Gamma 3 Mission and tell him to baptize the inhabitants. It's another thing if the inhabitants are Phobites, a race of giant hermaphroditic eggbeaters. Worse, what if a Phobite gets a testimony? As far as I know, there's no water for baptisms on P-G 3.

Things could get very complicated for me in the future. What if one of my daughters falls in love with a Wookie? There's no way I'm calling a bipedal Irish setter "son."

The Church may not consider this stuff worth fretting about but I do. Given my life, I'm more than a little concerned about what it's going to be like in the Extra-Terrestrial Kingdom.

# DEAR BROTHER KIRBY

BOUT A YEAR AGO, RELIGION NEWS SERVICE IN
Washington D.C. began syndicating some of
my columns to newspapers around the country. Since then, I've gotten feedback from Mormons
(and nons) living far from Zion. I thought you might
enjoy seeing what they had to say.

But first the rules. In order to protect the inno-
cent and ignorant, the writers here are identified
only by their initials. I've also taken the liberty of
making some spelling and grammar corrections. If by
some small chance you recognize a writer, tell them I
said "thanks."

  • "If what I read yesterday represents your
    real testimony of Jesus Christ and his
    church, why don't you find a church that

better suits you? I am sure there are many that would be willing to tolerate your babble." G.N., Phoenix, AZ.

• "I once thought Mormons were dangerous. But your column reveals that Mormons are really only just as crazy as the rest of us. Thank you for clearing that up." R.D., Indianapolis, IN.

• "Do you ever pray before you write? If you did, I am sure you would come to see the terrible damage you are doing to the only true church." A.R., Cheyenne, WY.

• "Your articles drive my mother-in-law and all of her church lady friends crazy. The enclosed five dollars is for the drink of your choice. Thank you, thank you, thank you." G.R., Salem, OR.

• "The rotten filth you write is proof that the LDS church needed enforcers like Porter Rockwell. If I get around you ever, you will be a sorry [expletive deleted]." Unsigned, Colorado Springs, CO.

• "You make me sick." D.V. Las Vegas, NV.

• "That was my sister in 'Five Kinds of Mormons.' She has been jack-booting around the church for years. It is wonderful to see that someone finally pegged her." P.M., Santa Fe, NM.

- "As a result of your shameful and untrue portrayal of the church, our good friends have stopped investigating the church." M.L., San Bernardino, CA.

- "Finally, a 'spokesman' for the LDS church that makes sense. My no-Mo friends roommates loved it. You make me proud to be Mo." L.M-D., Boise, ID.

- "How can your mother and father possibly sleep at night? For their sake if not the church's, please change your ways." Mrs. W. M., Seattle, WA.

- "[Deleted] you!!!" Anonymous, Flagstaff, AZ.

- "I am undecided as to your intent. Is it to make the church look false? Is it to mock your Heavenly Father? Are you just having fun? I expect an answer." A.H., Eugene, OR.

- "Curb, is that you? Jamie showed me the column in *The Sun*, man. Far out. Who writes it for you?" C. "Bugs" T., Ludlow, CA.

- "My friends and I would be willing to pay all expenses to have you attend our Gospel Doctrine class for just one Sunday. The teacher needs a dose of reality. Please say yes." K.Q., Santa Barbara, CA.

- "My wife was going to leave the church until we started reading your column. Now she wants to wait and see what happens to you. If the Brethren let you stay, maybe there is still hope for her." S.C., Sacramento, CA.

- "How is it that the church missed you when it cleaned out the other so-called 'intellectuals?' I would give anything to be your stake president for an hour." B.B., Los Angeles, CA.

# DYING TO DIE

B EEN THINKING ABOUT DEATH LATELY. MOSTLY
that it's about time I got a will, but also what
I want to happen if I become terminally ill or
lapse into a coma. Do I want my life pointlessly pro-
longed?

Knowing my family the way I do, the right kind of
will almost guarantees that this won't be a problem.
The plug is probably coming out of the wall five seconds after I'm no longer physically able to defend
myself.

Doesn't bother me. Prolonging the inevitable
when the end result is just a lot of pain and medical
bills is pointless. Frankly, if it really is my life, I want
most of the say when it comes time to calling it quits.

Most religions don't agree. According to them,
God alone decides when people should die. I'm not

so sure. Mainly because God seems to freelance a lot of this out to terrorists, the tobacco industry and the federal government. If God will let a drunk driver kill me, why can't I kill myself?

Opponents of legalizing euthanasia say such a law would send false messages to the elderly and teenagers. Legalizing euthanasia causes the elderly to believe that no one wants them around, while teenagers might look on it as a sign that life is more hopeless than they previously thought.

Actually, the reverse is true. Being old is hopeless, while being a teenager means that most people think you'd make better sense underground.

There's a down side to legalizing euthanasia; namely, that it would eventually become big business. Euthanasia centers will pop up all over, ranging from the chic to the cheap. Sears will have a booth next to their insurance stand, while 7-11 will sell little do-it-yourself pills that come with a free Big Gulp. Salesmen will come knocking on your door offering to kill you for 20 percent off.

Also, I wouldn't want to go to some discount suicide place where their idea of easing me into death would be to hit me with a hammer when I wasn't looking. I'd much rather check out in a nice, expensive hospital with lots of morphine.

Then there's the problem of timing. Not everyone who wants to die is all that rational. There have been times in my life when suicide illogically seemed the only option. Most memorably when I was eight and accidentally wet my pants on the playground in front of friends. If there'd been a Euth-Center across the street I would have trudged right over with my lunch money.

Finally, the government will undoubtedly come up with a Death Tax. You won't even be able to get away from them by dying like you can now. In fact, the government won't let you die until you fill out a form and give them a bunch of money. Heck, they'd keep you on life support in a federal penitentiary until you did.

Finally, who knows what kind of hoops religion would make people jump through. Mormons will probably have to have a temple recommend before killing themselves. I don't know about you, but the last group of people I want having any say in when and how I died is the Church's correlation committee.

When it's my time, I hope I go quick. If not, I'd be in favor of a law that allowed me to end my life with dignity by putting other people out of my misery.